The 8 BALL CAFE

*Stories of Adoption,
Addiction
and Redemption*

by
LORI CARANGELO

Access Press

contents

PART 3:
MORE ADDICTED ADOPTEES - 95

ADDENDUM - 121

RESOURCES and WEBSITES – 131

BIBLIOGRAPHY - 139

INDEX – 143

ABOUT THE AUTHOR - 145

The 8 Ball Café Bar
Huntington Park, California

PROLOGUE

Behind the 8 Ball

Lifetime prevalence rates of illicit substance use disorder (SUDs) are about **43% higher among adoptees** than non-adoptees:
- 41% for alcohol, compared to 27.5% among non-adoptees;
- 25.4% for adoptees, 16.1% for non-adoptees for nicotine;
- 2.9% for opioids, 1.3% for non-adoptees;
- 3.2% for cannabis for adoptees, 7.6% for non-adoptees.

--Patrick M. Burns, *"The Adjustment of Adoptees,"* Psychology Today, 3-31-15

The use of alcohol or drugs is often a means by which an adoptee calms or displaces anger—at society, parents, or his/her own "failure" to live up to others' expectation of "normalcy" despite the abnormal status of being adopted.

The 8 Ball Café was a bar that actually existed in Huntington Park, California, now disappeared from the landscape. At the 8 Ball Cafe, a deal was struck that forever changed a life. The 8 Ball Cafe is also symbolic of the moment and place where every adoption plan forever changed the course of an adopted person's life.

Unlike the game of 8-Ball, the players are not players by choice. As in the game, they end up "behind the 8 ball" of unreasonable adoption secrecy laws and learned behaviors. In the game of 8 Ball, there is a "triangle" in which the balls are racked before the game is played. In adoption, an adversarial triangle of competing interests is created — parents, adoptive parents, adoptees. In 8 Ball, the winner of a coin to take the first shot. Closed Adoption is also pretty much a "coin toss" or "crap shoot" in that a child is handed over to an unknown fate that no social worker, baby broker nor judge can predict nor guarantee. In 8 Ball, it is the opponent's right to ask for a "call shot" or "gentleman's call" if the next shot is not obvious, and there is a "legal break." An adoptee becomes a "legal fiction" requiring his/her "legal break" or lifelong separation from his biological family in order to be raised by strangers. The involved parties may have the right to ask questions when the adoptee attains adulthood, but the answers, if any, are scripted according politics, agency, social worker and state law as to mythical "child's best interests."

PART 1:

NOAH
STONE

*10"I used to be Snow White,
but I drifted."*
-Mae West

1.
GLADYS

Part of the tangled web of the puzzle that is Noah Stone was contributed by his adoptive mother, Gladys Gill, in the years before her death at age 85.

Gladys Marguerite Stone was raised a Mormon in Utah. Always praised for her striking looks, the raven-haired beauty always wore a pink bow in her hair, figure enhancing clothes, high heels that accentuated her shapely legs, and did not have to work hard at attracting male admirers. When barely legal age, she caught the eye of a wealthy California man who promised her a glamorous life. Instead, he abused her. But returning to Utah in embarrassment was out of the question. Taking only her clothes and her two dogs, she didn't have to think twice about leaving. Gladys headed for Alaska where a lot of men had been striking it rich on gold up there. Like the ladies with whom she shared a stately Victorian residence on the river, Gladys instinctively knew how to use her feminine attributes to separate the men from their cash. Prostituting earned her enough money to return to California, buy a comfortable home, and start her own knitting business. Still a "looker" although a chain smoker, she married Herb, a commercial refrigeration mechanic.

Herbert Gill, 49, was born in England. His wiry-thin build, facial "worry lines," and thinning brown hair peppered with gray, made him look older than his years. He made a decent living as a refrigeration mechanic and was successful at hiding the fact that he never learned to read. Herb met Gladys in 1955 at the knitting shop she owned on Gage, just off Long Beach Boulevard. He had a grown daughter by his first marriage. Herb adored Gladys. But his marriage proposal was hastened by the fact that her bookkeeping and management skills could help his business prosper while also protecting him from humiliation over his inability to read and write.

Gladys Gill at age 80, still wore a
pink bow in her hair.

"What you have become
is the price you paid
to get what you used to want."
-Mignon McLaughlin

2.
THE 8 BALL CAFÉ

It was a bright, warm January afternoon in 1962 - a typical Southern California day. Herb was on 24-hour call when he got a service call at the 8 Ball Cafe. When Herb wasn't working he sometimes also visited the 8 Ball for a drink, as it was close to his home and was a friendly place where the bartender and regulars knew him by name.

The conversation at the bar that day was about two children who had apparently been abandoned near the freeway between Huntington Park and Compton where Herb and Gladys lived. Distracted from repairing the bar's freezer, Herb dropped his tools and took a break to join the conversation. Gladys had been content at first to put off child bearing while they built the business. But by age 46 she had not been able to get pregnant and she was unwilling to share Herb's attention with his now grown daughter. Gladys wanted to "even the score" by having a child of their own—*even if they had to adopt one.* But a social worker advised Gladys that she and Herb would be considered "too old" to adopt, unless they found an older child, since it was harder to find homes for them -- Couples wanted newborns to raise "as if born to them."

Herb remarked to the men at the bar that if he had a chance, he and his wife "would adopt a child." A woman at the bar, a Latina who he hadn't seen before, took Herb aside and said she might know someone who could help him. The woman immediately got in touch with Kenneth Eugene Owens and they agreed to meet with Herb that evening at the 8 Ball Cafe. The night before, Owens had bought rounds of drinks for himself and the same woman Herb had encountered, until all his money was gone and his mood turned from one of celebration to lamenting the responsibilities ahead of him.

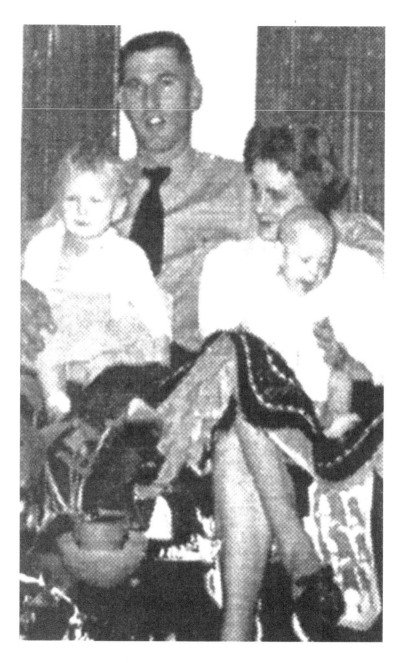

*Kenneth Owens, his wife, Jackie Sue, and
their children Susan and Kenneth Jr.*

Owens, born and raised in California, was a lean "24-years-young" man, just out of the Army Paratroopers, who had a pretty, blonde 17-year-old wife, Jackie Sue – and two kids. Jackie Sue was part Native American, born in Oklahoma during the Great Depression of 1930. Her pretty 2-year old blonde daughter, Susan, was a Treadwell, while their toddler, Kenneth Jr., was his biological son.

The Latina wasted no time in putting Owens in touch with the Gills who invited him to come over with the boy who Owens was considering adopting out as long as there was an interested couple. But Owens waited until his young wife was out of town before he presented himself with the boy.

The Gills found the smiling 3-1/2 year old Kenneth Owens Jr. to be so irresistibly cute, they wanted to formalize an adoption right away through their lawyer. The deal assured, Owens wasted no further conversation beyond agreeing to call back next day, and in the meantime *left the confused young Kenneth with the Gills.*

The next day, Owens called Gladys Gill, demanding $350 to keep Jackie Sue out of town long enough to formalize the adoption. Gladys and Herb refused to pay Owens, who then threatened he was coming to get his son back, saying he really didn't want to give him up for adoption, as a strategy to force the desperate couple to pay up.

But the Gills called the police, hoping to put pressure on Owens. The unexpected result was that Police Sergeant Edna Johnson instead took little Kenneth to McClaren Hall, and from there, the bewildered boy spent the next week with strangers in a foster home.

Gladys finally talked Owens into signing adoption papers, contending the father would be arrested for trying to "sell" the boy and that the boy would remain in foster care if he didn't let the Gills adopt him. But in the end they paid Owens the $350 he demanded, as they were unsure what would become of the little boy if they and Owens could not reach an agreement.

Sergeant Edna Johnson then arranged to meet Jackie Sue at the 8 Ball Cafe. Johnson was supposed to give Jackie Sue $50, provided by

Gladys, "for rent money" and convince her to sign adoption papers. Instead, Johnson pocketed the cash and began providing Jackie Sue with a pack of cigarettes per day which proved to be enough of a lure to keep her in town until the adoption plan was fulfilled. Jackie Sue did go to the 8 Ball Cafe with her little Susan in tow to receive from Sergeant Johnson the promised pack of cigarettes every day until the papers were ready to sign - papers that Johnson said would allow a *"temporary"* placement and *"avoid charges of neglect."* When Jackie Sue did sign, it was with a big "X" -- s h e had never been taught to read and write and so could not have known what she was signing, only what Johnson alleged it to be.

Sergeant Johnson even saw to it that Jackie Sue and Owens each showed up separately at the offices of attorneys Hansen and Bunnett in nearby Southgate. Attorney John W. Bunnett made sure the Owenses and the Gills had appointment times at least a day apart, lest they run into each other. It was then February, but it would not be until July that the filed petition for permanent adoption would commence in the Superior Court at Southgate. In the meantime, Jackie Sue began to suspect she had been tricked and was speeding to Johnson's office to demand return of her boy... *when a traffic accident put her into a coma.* By the time J a c k i e S u e awoke from her coma, her children were *gone.*

The Gills had been advised that an adoption is not final for a period of approximately one year from the date of approved petition, and the Bureau of Adoptions still needed to do a "home study" and file their Supplemental Report. Gladys wasn't worried. She felt she had duly impressed the social worker who spent no more than five minutes inspecting the Gills' stately two-story Huntington Park home, and verifying Herb's good income. The Gills' "fitness" as parents was already established since they were already fostering the shy, quiet boy who appeared respectfully well-mannered and "adjusted" to his situation when, in fact, he was traumatized by the woman who was telling him she was now his "mother" and that he must forget that he already had a mother.

The process was completed without a hitch.

3.
THE DONE DEAL

Gladys believed she had once caught a brief glimpse of the boy's mother at the back of the courtroom, but her curiosity about Jackie Sue was forgotten the moment the judge's gavel banged, asserting his Order to seal the boy's original birth certificate. A "legally falsified" birth certificate substituted Gladys and Herbert Gill's names for Jackie and Kenneth Owens as the child's parents on his date of birth. Thus, Kenneth Owens was "reborn" as "Herbert Kent Gill."

According to Gladys:

> "We were told he was one of four children before his mother was twenty. The first child, Susan, went to Jackie's parents in Oklahoma. He was the second, born in Bakersfield, August 1, 1958. And the other two had been already adopted from the hospital. The father said when Jackie was hospitalized from the traffic accident he could not afford to pay someone to take care of the boy. I don't believe he was really married to the mother but the boy was his child. He had said that the mother would take the boy along when she went to bars and leave him in the car until closing time."

Gladys went on about the boy:

> "We were strangers to Kent (that's what she preferred to call him), but he never cried, never asked when he was going home, nor where his mother was. He called every woman "mother," but he referred to his father as "the bad man." We never asked about the odd looking bruises on his skinny legs and arms, and no family background was ever offered us. He weighed 28 pounds and looked as if he might break easily. Kent did not talk of where he had lived nor of any people he knew. He was not toilet trained and would not say when he had to go to the bathroom. I put diapers on him at night and he did not wet. But if I left them off, he did."

17

Three days after "Kent" was placed with the Gills, Gladys had a medical emergency and was hospitalized, and so left him in care of her sister and brother-in-law. They upset the boy by calling him *"stupid,"* a word he thought was even worse than it was for a little boy to hear. He became even more quiet and withdrawn after that.

Rarely did the Gills have people over to the house and never did they leave Kent alone when they went out. Never. He either went to Miss Esther down the street, or was with the Gills. So he spent his youth around a lot of adults.

Whenever they drove through various neighborhoods with him in the car, he always claimed he recognized his previous family's house but also pointed out other homes he claimed to have lived in at one time or other.

Kent began running away from the Gills for as long as they can remember. In fact, he was never in their home for a full year.

The Gills' mailman remembered often hearing violent sounding arguments when he delivered mail through the front door slot at the Gills' home. But Gladys denied that Herb ever beat her, as her first husband did. According to Gladys,

> "Kent misunderstood. Herb and I were 'just kidding around' and the next thing we knew, *Kent was pointing a rifle at Herb!*"

Despite that, as of July 31, 1963, the adoption was legally finalized, Gladys remained nervous. She feared she'd made a mistake. Would Herb ever really accept Kent as his son? He rarely became involved with the boy, except in later years when he would attend his son's special swimming meets now and then. Herb belonged to the Shriners, Al Malaikah Temple in Los Angeles, Scottish Rite Temple, the Elks, Moose Lodge, and the Foresters which was more than enough distraction and excuse for avoiding becoming involved with the troubled boy. Gladys also feared that Herb's attention was being diverted back to his biological daughter because Herb was afraid that his already grown daughter was upset about his having adopted a young child. There *was* jealousy, but it was Herb who, instead of being more attentive, broke off all contact with his own daughter who later claimed that Gladys had manipulated the breakup and would not allow her father to call her.

18

His daughter's memory of her own and Kent's abuse at the hands of the Gills supports their adopted son's depiction of his young life:

> "That woman is *evil!* She not only threw Kent into the same cage with the family dogs, she whipped us both with her riding crop!"

*"Trapped inside my brain, the child who will always
want to come out and play;
his world: where children hide,
and fears for all, run high."*
-Noah Stone

4.
TROUBLED GENIUS

Gladys shared snippets of her adopted son's childhood:

> "At age five, Kent attended kindergarten at a private school,
> but at the end of the year, the teacher said he was too
> immature to go into first grade and should repeat
> kindergarten or go to first grade at a public school."

Because Gladys was having trouble enrolling Kent in first grade, when he
was seven she brought him for testing to Marion Davis Neuro-Psychiatric
Institute (NPI) Clinic at UCLA *and he was made to reside there eleven months.*

Gladys bragged, "After one month of testing, the clinical psychologist
stated that this boy had a *very high IQ — genius level."*

But Gladys seemed oblivious to how painfully long an eleven month
separation can be for a seven-year-old boy, nor that he was forced to take
a strong "anti-depressant" drug to calm his "hyperactivity" – the term used to
diagnose young adoptees who had anxiety over separation and loss of their
biological families.

> "He came home on weekends, and my husband and I had
> one-hour sessions, once a week, with the social worker and
> psychiatrist. All of the staff liked him and I believe he quit
> stealing for a time," Gladys explained.

But Kent had a different memory of the UCLA's NPI clinic:

> "I was acting up, as kids do at that age, and I guess a bit too
> much for their liking. I had evidently done something so
> bad that I was strapped to a bed and given a shot — of what, I
> have no idea..

21

I went to sleep. When I woke up, I was still strapped down and had even wet the bed. No one had bothered to change the sheets or un-strap me for the longest time. Funny how you remember such things. I know why my adoptive parents put me there. They had no idea what a "hyper" kid was about. But the doctors knew! And to this day, I hate doctors."

Gladys referred to what she called her son's "lifelong kleptomania." She wouldn't let him play at friends' homes "because he always brought home some trinkets he claimed were given to him but which he lifted." Gladys went along on his first paper route "to make sure he didn't have an opportunity to 'case' homes in the process." She didn't see his problems as *adoption-and-separation-related* "because never lived with us for very long at a time."

Kent found a release for his anxiety:

> "UCLA's NPI Clinic had a pool... and I used to go out and watch the other kids swim. Then one day I asked if I could try. I was only seven and didn't know how to swim, nor had I even been in a pool. But as soon as I got in, it was like a world I had 'come home to.' I remember that I really didn't need any instruction — I just started swimming."

For a time, Gladys thought daily swims would dissipate the boy's "hyperactivity" and his problems.

> "But," she said, "the principal, Mrs. Swinefest, kept sending him home after he had been in school for only 15 minutes to an hour. She would then tell me I should "have him *put away* because he should be *locked up* the rest of his life. About that time, he started stealing again. I talked to Dr. Brackelmann who we had started seeing once a week. He told me not to pay any attention to Mrs. Swinefest. I put Kent into public school but he was always coming home with some little thing that did not belong to him. He had also begun sneaking out of his second story window and down a trellis "to go see downtown." I was never sure why — whether he looking for his family or just running away from us."

Sometimes he managed to climb up to the roof to "just sit and gaze up at the stars, to *feel free*," he said, because Gladys kept such a close eye on him. To keep him from slipping out the window and hurting himself, the Gills installed bars on his bedroom window, locked his door at night, and checked on him frequently by means of a peephole in the door.

Believing he was "simply hyperactive," when he was in second and third grades, Gladys took Kent to swimming lessons *twice a day*—once in the daytime and once in the evening, "to tire him out enough to sleep," she said. He was the first kid to win their gold medal in gymnastics since the program began fourteen years before. He accomplished this while in and out of Juvenile Hall. The gymnastics coach said he was a natural athlete, but after a short time he would start acting up.

Gladys added,

> "The gymnastics coach wanted to work with him and asked permission to '*hypnotize*' him. I asked the doctor about it. He said 'Go ahead, but I don't think he can do it.' The coach tried but was unsuccessful. We quit the Athletic Club because he started fourth grade in public school. But a week later they started a 'handicapped class' and we enrolled him in that."

Determined to tutor her adopted son herself, Gladys devised a "game" she played with him on a drive to the bank one day. She'd make him remove an article of clothing for every incorrect answer to a math problem. By the time they reached the bank, the little boy was completely naked and humiliated but no more a math whiz.

From 1966 to 1970 Kent was placed in schools for the "*emotionally* handicapped" and learning disabled, as well as classes for the *physically* handicapped. He was dyslexic, and continued to steal items of no significant value, "from pencils to an old pillowcase."

In 1971, when Kent was 13, he attended Gage Junior High for two or three months and then was back at Juvenile Hall.

Gladys continued:

> "Police Sergeant Edna Johnson, the same person who arranged our son's adoption, and who, by then, knew us well because of Kent's many attempts to run away from home, advised us to put Kent in a 'reform school.'
>
> When she did bring him to Las Padrinos Juvenile Hall, the Director said to me, 'Are you *sure* about doing this?' because all Kent had done was try to run away from us. I talked to Dr. Brackleman and he recommended Camarillo State Hospital, saying 'They will work with his behavior and schooling.'"

Gladys was, at least for a time, in favor of committing her son. She did not know that, for decades, mental hospitals in the United States were not only *warehouses* for the insane but also for epileptics, alcoholics, the indigent elderly, unruly women, *and orphans.*

Gladys went on:

> "Edna Johnson then advised me to make him a ward of the court. I regret that we did so. That's when they sent him to the mental hospital at Camarillo. That was a mistake."

"Twenty percent of adolescents in drug rehabilitation and in residential substance abuse treatment programs are adopted."
-National Adoption Center (NAC) Philadelphia, PA

5.
ADOPTED, ABUSED, ADDICTED

Drugs had already become a large part of Kent's life from age seven, when psychiatrists began giving him anti-depressants.

In Kent's words:

> "Prescription anti-depressants, given to me since age seven got me started on my lifelong addiction. Later, the feelings from "good drugs" (street drugs) always seemed a lot better than the "bad drugs" (prescribed drugs). I was always trying to attain the feeling that I could cope with the world — or, as I called it, 'The Living'."

At Camarillo State Hospital, he was put on drugs the day he arrived, October 5, 1971. He was given Mellaril, (thioridazine), a powerful anti-psychotic, four times a day.

Gladys worried:

> "His schooling got worse, also his behavior, and, in about three months, he ran away three times with someone else that was in his ward. He forgot everything he had learned and became very hateful when he came home on weekends. They would always send the pills home with him, and if I forced him to take them he would sleep all the time and be very mean when he woke up."

Kent remembers:

> "My first time at Camarillo, Mom drove me up there. It took about three hours to go through the intake crap and be

25

admitted to Unit 3. Standing there, watching her drive away, I was again feeling abandoned, but at the same time happy to be rid of her. New place, new people, that was cool. I always found it easy to meet and get along.

I remember a couple of the kids. There was 'Big Fat Tommy' who been there for years. When I think of Tommy, I feel so sad for him. I don't think he really belonged there. His people just threw him out like so much trash. He was big—six feet tall and so fat that his t-shirts never fit him because his belly would always hang out—a funny sight. At night, he would lay on his side and rock himself to sleep. That's when I started doing the same thing when it's hard to sleep. I really hope he's okay these days.

Walter—Oh, Walter! This kid spent more time in straps than free of them. Walter would go off about something and then all these nurses would hold him down, give him a shot and strap him down to his bed. He had his own room, whereas the rest of us were in dorms. I don't know why I remember Walter so much, since we never saw that much of him, because he was kept asleep on meds. When he was awake and not going off, he was okay. Walter had a very loud, high pitched laugh and didn't have many friends, except me and Tommy. I have a gut feeling that Walter was either eventually killed or killed himself. Poor Walter.

There were dances at the girls' unit. The music was 'Blood, Sweat and Tears,' but I would only dance the slow dances. I remember kissing a lot with my girlfriend, Karen, between classes and after school. The first sex I had was at the Camarillo kids' units. I think I lasted all of twenty seconds. It may have been fast but it was damn good."

He also recounted:

"I ran away four times, my first time at Camarillo—each time with another kid, and we walked a long way. The second time at Camarillo I used State cars to escape.

I was also hateful toward Gladys because she was always on me about what she wanted me to do and be. She was very bossy and controlling. If I didn't do something right, or her way, she would yell and make me do it *over and over and over again.*"

Gladys never questioned whether the prescribed drugs were what was worsening his behaviors:

"He tore all the wallpaper off the wall in his room, slashed the upholstery in the car, wandered through the house at night while we slept, carrying lit candles to the attic. We didn't know then that he was suffering severe side effects from the drug."

Edna Johnson, the same juvenile officer who had taken Kent to McClaren Juvenile Hall when he was three and a half, later saw the change it had made in him and advised the Gills:

"That is no place for Kent. Get him out, but place him where he would still get treatment."

Just before Christmas, 1972, Kent was again at Las Padrinos Juvenile Hall. The police report stated:

"Said minor is beyond the control of his parents with whom he resides in that on or about December 23, 1972, minor left home without parental permission by breaking and climbing out of his bedroom window and his whereabouts remained unknown until December 24, 1972." Reflecting on those times, Kent would later realize:
"Christmas always felt somehow empty for me, no matter what anyone did to try to make it a happy occasion. I would wonder what *my real mother* was doing. Did she think of me at Christmas? It was the same on my birthday—there were no mementos in the family album about the day I was born, or of the people I was born to. Hell, I couldn't even prove I *existed* before age three, since there were no photos, no records of my true identity."

In 1974, his *new probation officer*, Lillian Ferguson, unfamiliar with all that had happened to the boy, then placed him in a foster home in El Monte. He was removed from there within six days and placed in East Lake Central Juvenile Hall.

A month later, Ferguson took him to Roscilli's Boy's Ranch, where he and another boy ran away after five days. He was then sent to Ken Ruffcorn's home on part of Roscilli's Ranch, where he didn't get along, and was then sent to the Willard Home.

By May, 1974, Kent was on the road again. On May 9th, Ferguson brought him back home to the Gills to await a hearing on June 19,1974.

On July 6 to August 13th, he was back to Central Juvenile Hall.

Then to Camp Paige. He didn't like it there, either, and was on the run from August 14th to 17th.

Gladys took him back to Camp Paige and they took him back to Central Juvenile Hall.

Kent was a ping-pong ball between his adoptive parents, the system, and his own need to get away but with no place he could stand to stay that would keep him.

By the end of 1974, he was again committed to Camarillo State Hospital.

He ran away from Camarillo, but was caught on February 8, 1975, and was sent to McClaren Hall where he was first brought, sixteen years before, to secure his adoption.

He was sent home to the Gills again and went back to the Lynwood Swim team and to start the school year.

But on February 26 he was arrested by Southgate Police for Burglary and sent to USC Medical Center.

Noah believes: *"I conned them into thinking I was nuts."*

April 1, 1975, he was back at Camarillo State Mental Hospital for a third time.

Five days later, he ran away to the Gills' home, but left home "to see an old girlfriend," leaving Gladys and Herb to wonder when he had *time* to find a girlfriend.

He was back and forth, and living on the streets until arrested again April 29, 1975, and sent back to Camarillo for the fourth time.

He ran away from Camarillo again, and was picked up by Huntington

Park Police.

Back at Camarillo, he wrote:

> "Dear Mom and Dad, I'm not crazy. But if you want to see me in a place that can do me some good, then do it. Put me in one so I can get some help from someone. I hope I can show you that I can be someone in this world, make some money, and help you and Dad to get settled in a good place that I can get."

Based partly on fact and partly on his fantasy of the brother he might have had, on August 27, 1975, psychiatrist Marshall S. Cherkas, MD, wrote to Patricia A. McFarlane, Deputy Public Defender, about Kent:

> "He believes he has a natural brother named Don Chafe who is now at Norwalk Youth Authority and is reportedly sixteen or seventeen year of age. He knows nothing of his natural parents' whereabouts. He indicates some *considerable resentment about being adopted*. He feels that being with his adoptive mother is like World War III, that he is somehow unable to live up to her expectations. Intellectually, he appears to be in the "average" range. This is a seventeen year old boy who appears somewhat younger than his age, and although cooperative, he definitely seems *poorly in contact with reality*."

The Diagnosis: "Schizophrenic reaction of adolescence, borderline psychotic."

Cherkas also opined:

> "Some of his impulsive reactions may be related to LSD flashbacks, probably more likely tied in with the chaotic and confused states he suffers when he is mildly depressed and obviously needs concerned direction and limit setting. He will definitely need long term psychotherapy in one form or other."

During the first three decades of his life, he sampled each of the following:

- KEROSENE and GLUE VAPORS– which can cause liver damage, bone damage, sudden death;

- SEDATIVES-- Quaalude (methaqualone), Amylbarbital with Secobarbital ("rainbows," "double trouble"), Secobarbital/Seconal ("reds,"), Phenobarbital ("yellows") — which can cause convulsions and death;

- HALLUCINOGENS-- DMT, MDH, morninglory seeds, LSD or "acid" — which can cause psychoses, "bad trips," irrational behavior, chromosome abnormalities, flashbacks;

- CANNABIS-- marijuana or "grass," "weed" and hashish, THC — which can possibly cause mental habituation, lack of motivation, neurosis, accidents, delayed maturing, flashbacks, and temporary psychoses;

- STIMULANTS--including Noah's drug of choice, methamphetamine, ("meth," "speed," "crystal," "crank") — which can cause mental habituation, psychoses, hypertension, hyper-metabolic state, brain hemorrhage, arthritis, aggressiveness, paranoia; Noah's method of choice became "mainlining" ("shooting up speed" intravenously) hich frequently brings complications including: hepatitis, cellulitis, bacterial sepsis, bacterial endocarditis, thrombophlebitis, pulmonary embolism, pulmonary infarction, lung abscesses, arteritis, gangrene...

....and sudden death.

One of Noah's many prison tattoos.

"Sealed records are a from of child abuse."
--Sharon Kaplan, BSW, MS,
adoptive parent,
"Parenting Resources," Tustin, CA

6.
IDENTITY CRISIS

At the age of legal adulthood, when teenagers are thought to experience an "identity crisis," Kent Gill took on a new identity -- one he chose himself, as adoptees often do – From that day forward, he's been "Noah Stone." But Gladys continued to call him "Kent," the name *she* chose for him.

Noah and Gladys never agreed on just how "Noah Stone" came about:

> "As for how I chose my name, I didn't get 'Noah Stone' from Mom's Stone family Bible, as Gladys tells it. I was actually first called 'Noah' back in 1975 or '76 while running on the streets of Hollywood. Some people just started calling me that and it stuck. Then, in 1984, when I was in Tracy Prison, I thought about changing my last name to Stone. I didn't know that was Gladys' parents' name until I came home and saw it in the big dictionary that was once her father's, not in her Bible."

Noah was a ward of the court until 1976 when he was eighteen. Up until then, he had also lived at Lakeside Lodge at Lake Elsinore where he was punished with ping-pong paddles and poked in his ribs by a Black Belt karate counselor.

He ran away with another boy whose stepfather was a homosexual. The boy took Noah to another homosexual in Long Beach, a 50-year old ex-convict who gave them a little money. They were picked up the next day on the pier by police, put in jail, and then returned to Lakeside Lodge. Gladys later wondered whether her boy had been molested in Long Beach and whether it was the first time. If Noah had been sexually molested, he wasn't talking, and the Gills weren't asking. According to Gladys:

"Mr. Gill and I were not allowed to visit Kent for three months. Yet they let the other boy's stepfather go there every weekend and take the boys home — the boys who did not have parents to come see them. Kent ran away again.

There was to be another hearing but the probation officer did not have Kent present and told the judge to release Kent *to me*. Mr. Gill was busy with his own business, which was commercial refrigeration. He serviced markets, restaurants, bars, flower shops and also air-conditioning.

We are *responsible* parents."

Yet the Gills were constantly relinquishing their responsibility to governmental authority.

On February 25,1977, Noah wrote to his parents while in the custody of the NRCC "WINTU " psychiatric program:

"The people on staff were okay, but they all love to give the kids that little drug. I had to run because I couldn't find myself there. And I couldn't find myself at home either. When I was little, I didn't run to 'find myself,' just to find someone to play with... If you wanted to see and be with me bad enough, you would."

In 1978, Dr. David Kirschner's paper, *"Adopted Child Syndrome,"* was published, but it would be another 10 years before the general public would read that 14-year-old Patrick DeGelleke burned down his adoptive parents' home, killing them, in his effort to fake his own death so he would be "free to find his mother, in *"How the Adoption System Ignites a Fire"* (by Betty Jean Lifton, New York Times, 3-1-86) and "Adopted Child Syndrome" was offered by DeGelleke's defense lawyer as a mitigating circumstance that saved only DeGelleke but also Patrick Campbell, Matthew Heikkila, and several other adoptees from the Death Penalty and won Degelleke his release at legal age. "Adopted Child Syndrome," while not universally accepted, is commonly considered to be a set of behaviors observed in to varying degrees in adoptees, and that *all adoptees* are *"at risk"* for developing them.

34

The eight "Adopted Child Syndrome (ACS)" behaviors include:

- conflict with authority, truancy;
- preoccupation with excessive fantasy;
- pathological lying, manipulative;
- stealing;
- running away;
- learning difficulties, under achievement,
- lack of impulse control, including sexual acting out;
- setting fires

ACS personalities are characterized by lack of impulse control, low frustration tolerance, manipulation, deceptive charm, shallowness of attachment, and an absence of normal guilt ("remorse") or anxiety about one's deeds.

Noah exhibited all of these behaviors following his adoption.

On May 1, 1978, Kent wrote Gladys:

> "Dear Mom, I am really sorry for putting you through hell all your life. Now you can live in peace for the rest of your life because you don't have to worry about me anymore because I'm going to get out of your life forever. All my love, Kent. PS: Please remember me as I was when I was three or before I went bad."

On June 9, 1978, a Confidential Report, ICR 5805, by O.L. Gericke, MD, Highland, California, to the Office of Public Defender regarding Herbert Kent Gill, summarizes Noah's drug history, *omits Adopted Child Syndrome,* and recommends brain wave analysis at Riverside County General Hospital, and concludes:

> "It can only be deduced that in this important period of his life, the first 3-1/2 years, he was not able to form any emotional ties with parental figures and this caused behavioral problems."

"Do you have to be truant, steal cars,
get into juvenile detention homes,
or drop out of school for people to realize
that you need to have someone tell you
about your origins?"
-Jean Paton, MA, MSW
Adoptee, Social Worker, and
"Mother" of The Open Records Movement

7.
SILLY CRIMES, SERIOUS TIME

In "People v. Herbert Kent Gill" (CR 58085, July 20,1978, Superior Court, County of Riverside, at Indio, California) -- regarding Noah's May 25, 1978 offense, "Unlawful Taking of an Automobile," a felony—it states:

> "In an interview conducted at the Indio jail, Noah Stone admitted to drinking alcohol and taking controlled substances prior to his taking the Toyota pickup truck.... that he began hallucinating while he was wandering around Palm Desert. The Defendant states he didn't feel he would be caught because he planned on returning the vehicle once he returned from Los Angeles.'"

From September 19, 1981 to October 3, 1981, Noah was back on anti-depressants at Mesa Vista Hospital, San Diego, on referral from L.K. Pratum, Rancho Mirage. Mesa Vista's psychiatric report on Noah reads:

> "The background history is *pathogenomonoic* as to the psychopathology, in as much as this was *a rejected child or rejected infant.* He was irritated when telling about his family, particularly his mother. His voice would get louder and there were implications of the intense hatred-love relationship. Asendin, an anti-depressant, seemed to produced a beneficial effect, so initially, he was exposed to the milieu drug therapy at the hospital, plus daily psychotherapy. He expressed anger."

Final Diagnosis: "Dysthymic reaction, drug abuse, antisocial personality behavior."

Doctors at Mesa Vista were the first to suggest that *Noah's adoption and unknown pre-adoption history* had significant bearing on his adult behaviors – a surprising event, since it would be another five years, before anyone in the medical community would publicly acknowledge "Adopted Child Syndrome (ACS)" behaviors, identical to Noah's.

Despite over two decades of police and doctors' reports mentioning Noah's abuse and neglect by his adoptive parents, no charges of child abuse or neglect were ever filed against the Gills.   Noah's outcome was instead merely blamed on Noah.

September 23, 1981, there was a report by Charles Gable, MD, Mesa Vista:

"He was adopted at a price of $350 by his now elderly parents when he was 3-1/2. He says he remembers being in Juvenile Hall at age 3 and believes his troubles began then. He has been in and out of jails many times. He is now under indictment for Burglary and Auto Theft in two different places. Once when he was released, he stole the same car for which he had been jailed initially. He complained that he has grown up with locks and bars. He said his adoptive mother locked him in a closet, locked him in his room at night, and beat him on the legs with a riding crop when he tried to run away. He reported that she made audio tapes of him crying and punished and ridiculed him in public. He is more angry with her than with his father and has threatened her life. He explained that his adoptive mother and uncle had called him 'stupid' and he felt this has had a lifelong effect on him. He has since done 'what stupid people do' as a kind of masochistic punishment of self. He reads horror novels and science fiction and thought he must read at college level by now.   Living with a hyperactive child is wearing and his adoptive mother was 49 when he was three. She may have lacked the stamina and patience required to deal with a child offered for sale by his natural parents.

The failure to bond presents continuing complications to his early and present development. *His auditory attention span is equivalent to that of nine year old children."*

Although Mesa Vista provided the most accurate appraisal of the root of his problems, Noah was unimpressed:

"Mesa Vista didn't really do all that many tests on me, and at the time I went there I was wanted by the cops in Santa Barbara and I knew that Mesa Vista would not tell the cops I was there. By law, they can't. So I was free a little longer."

Since attaining legal age of 21 in 1978, in accordance with California law, Noah was beyond reach of Juvenile Authority, foster homes, and Gladys. From then on, he racked up a criminal "rap" sheet and did "serious time," some of which he utilized to obtain his G.E.D. high school equivalency at Deuel Vocational Institution in California State Prison at Tracy, California, where there was an undated notation as to suspicion of "possible contraband substance," and the one documented positive test for cocaine on May 28-29, 1986 -- yet none of the arrests nor convictions on Noah's record were for "drug use." He was always charged with misdemeanor or "felony thefts" and burglaries, not drug use or possession, and so his sentences never included mandatory drug treatment of any kind.

"Rap sheet" for "GILL, Kent Herbert," (aka Herbert Burnett, Herbert Kent Gill, Noah Gill, Noah Kent Gill, Herb Gill):

2-27-76, PD Southgate. Released to Public Guardian's office.
1-20- 77, CYS, Norwalk. Failure to obey an order. Field placement.
6-23-77, S.O. Riverside, escape
3-15-78, paroled.
5-2- 78, S. 0. Riverside, taking a vehicle.
8-3-78, CA Dept of Corrections, Chino. Theft of vehicle. Term 2 years.
9-25-78, discharged
9-12-79, paroled to Riverside County.
3-12-81, discharged. Possible contraband substance.
10-26-81, S.O. San Jose. Vehicle without CONS.
11-12-81, CA Dept of Corrections, received for diagnosis from Santa
    Clara County. Term 90-day placement.

1-14-82, discharge.

3-4-82, CA Dept of Corr, theft of vehicle in Santa Clara. Term 3 years

4-29-82, CA Dept of Corr, additional commitment from Santa Barbara County. Term 2 years.

9-8-83, paroled to Santa Clara County.

12-15-83, CA Dept of Corr/ Chino, Parole violation RTC./ Term begins with Prior 3-4-82.

3-7-84, Paroled to San Diego

4-19-84, CA Dept. Of Corrections, Chino, parole violation R T C ; Term begins with Prior 3-4-82.

4-1-85, Paroled to San Diego County

4-25-85, CA Dept. Of Corrections, Chino, parole violation, Chino, Term begins with Prior 3-4-82.

6-17-85, Paroled to San Diego County

1-26-86, Arrested by members of Lima, Ohio Sheriff's Office for harboring a fugitive—known drug dealer. Subject and his *wife* arrested for Obstructing Justice; pled guilty; Term 3 months.

5-13-86, Revise prior notation

5-28-86, Test results returned positive for cocaine; admitted to charge; showed no injection sites; said he injected himself with speed (amphetamines) at least 3 times.

5-28-86 State of Ohio v. Noah Stone: Obstructing Justice (Felony); Obstructing Justice (misdemeanor); confinement in Allen County Jail 3 months; fine $100; pled guilty.

5-29-86, Arrested by Riverside County Sheriffs Office for Burglary; he didn't remember doing the burglary; he remembered shooting up speed and then remembers being arrested, but admitted stealing the items upon arrest; discovered hiding in some trees. When we attempted to arrest him, he threatened to slit his throat. Had two hunting knives with a blade longer than 2 inches.

6-12-86: Changing residence without notifying parole agent; subject turned himself in to Indio Parole Office; he was not arrested at the time but was arrested one day later on other charges; he stated he was just tired of being on parole.

Also noted in that 1986 report was the following by Indio Parole Officer, Joseph Leggett:

"We are dealing with an individual whose only consideration is his immediate gratification of his needs and he does not

40

consider the consequences of his actions. Mr. Gill has been in the system since he was a young boy. Besides prison, he has been in a number of mental institutions for emotional problems. Unfortunately, it seems, Mr. Gill has no intention of changing his lifestyle."

A few years later, Leggett referred to Noah as a "career criminal" and "beyond rehabilitation," in his opinion.

7-9-86: Noah was in trouble again. Municipal Court, Palm Springs, People v. Herbert Gill, MCR9896. Honorable Phillip LaRoca, presiding judge determined:

"The victim identified Noah as the man coming out of his house and again later when he spotted him across from my house in the trees... He was just sitting there."

Officer Craig Bender testified:

"I had asked him [Noah] to come out of the bushes so I could talk to him and he had a couple of long knives, like a survival knife and a kitchen knife; he pointed those at me. I pointed my gun at him and then he put the knives up to his throat and then that's kind of the position we were in when we were having the conversation. He said he didn't want to come out because he was afraid he would be hurt. He said several times that all he wanted to do was go back East *to see his birth family in Ohio.* I asked him why he was so afraid. He said he was on parole and had just burglarized the house across the way on Merle Street. He appeared to be hiding. He was sitting down with his legs drawn up to his chest and he was holding his shirt up/hiding his head. And then he put the knives up to his neck again... Later, on arrest, in his wallet was discovered *his birth certificate.*"

Noah always confessed to crimes and plea bargained via public defenders who did not adequately represent him. He repeatedly volunteered that he was "*sold* for adoption," which was a crime, yet no one suggested opening his adoption file nor investigating Noah's allegation of child trafficking because it happened so long ago.

41

Addiction *and violence* are also often the side-effects of *legally prescribed* substances. The federal Drug Enforcement Administration (DEA) classified Ritalin in the same category as Morphine, Opium, and Cocaine. Littleton, Colorado was most notorious for doling out Ritalin to kids, particularly in wealthy suburbs, as well as in public supported foster care. Long term effects of Ritalin are still being debated in the wake of the Columbine High School shootings in Littleton and similar mass shooting incidents nationwide. When prescribed for adoptees, Ritalin, Mellaril, and other mood altering drugs may lead to addictions and violence against themselves and others. Joan Kauffman, Ph.D., Andres Martin, M.D., Dennis Charney, M.D., Yale University staff from the Department of Psychiatry and Child Study Center, (in their Letter to the Editor, published in Newsweek, at the time of the Columbine shootings), contend:

> "There are preliminary data to suggest that the biological changes associated with early adversity can be prevented through exposure to consistent nurturing," but this doesn't seem to be the case with adoptees whose adoptive parents allegedly provided the recommended ingredients."

According to another article, *"Getting a Hold on Rage, Some Adoptive Parents Find Love Alone Isn't the Answer — Now They're Upset That The State Won't Help Pay For a Promising New Treatment"* (Jack Kresnak, Detroit Free Press, 6-25-95):

> *"There is no formula for making a stranger's child live up to their adoptive parents' expectations. To a child, the burden of such expectations translates as abuse.* The aforementioned Newsweek letter ends with "Not *all* traumatized children become violent, and there are no simple answers to explain *why* some youths kill."

In his book *"Reclaiming Our Children: A Healing Solution for a Nation In Crisis"* (Perseus, 2000) Peter R. Breggin, MD, a private practitioner in Bethesda, Maryland, presents strong evidence that psychiatric drugs commonly *cause* psychoses and aggression in children, and that they probably contributed to individual cases of school violence. In his best selling

42

"Talking Back to Prozac" and *"Talking Back to Ritalin,"* he makes specific recommendations for improving family and school life based on sound psychological and ethical principles. But what if the "family" is a "shadow family"—a prohibition to the child under the unsound psychology and unethical practice perpetuated by closed adoption? What if the child does not accept his adoptive parents as "family?" Can any drug treatment change that, or just compound the problem?

The following narcotics are grouped according to how they increase and decrease sensory attention and motor activity:

- UPPERS - [High Activity; High Action] — stimulants, hypermaniacs, amphetamine ("speed," "meth," "crank,"),

- "crystal," "whites," "bennies," "black beauties"), amyl nitrate, caffeine, cocaine, methyldiamphetamine, methylpheidate, pemoline, Benezedene (TM), Dexedrine (TM) ("dexies"), Clyert (TM), Prozac (TM), Ritalin (TM), methadrine (TM), Preludin (TM).

- CONFUSERS - [High Activity; Low Attention] — Convulsants Synthetics, Hallucinogens, Psychodelics, mescaline, psilocybin, lycergic diethylamide, PCP, DMT, LSD.

- CALMERS - [Low Activity; High Attention] — Tranquilizers, Narcopleptics, butylprophenanone, dibenzoxazepone, lithium, nicotine, tetrahydracanabinal, phenothiazine, Cibalth (TM), Haldol (TM), Loxitane (TM), Moban (TM), Thorazine (TM) ("barbs," "goofballs, "dolls"), Seconal ("reds") Phenobarbital ("blues," "yellows,"), Amylbarbital-Secobarbital ("rainbows").

- DOWNERS - [Low Activity; Low Attention] Depressants, Anesthetics, alcohol, barbiturates, carbonate opiates, Pentathol (TM), Nembutol (TM), Methadone (TM), Amytal, Barbitol (TM), Demerol (TM), Xanax (TM), BuSpar (TM), Phenobarbital (TM).

Children who "graduate" from prescribed drugs to street drugs find that "Uppers," such as cocaine, can give a "high-high," such as being both more active and more attentive as long as the intoxication lasts. "Downers" such as heroin, in contrast, gives a "low-low," such as being both less active and less attentive as long as one is under the influence. "Calmers," like marijuana, give a "low-high," where activity level is low while attention is high. "Confusers," such as LSD, give a "high-low," where one is very active but has great difficulty paying attention to surroundings.

"Something there is in us that doesn't love a wall,
That wants to tear it down."
-Robert Frost, "The Mending Wall"

8.
THE SEARCH

In 1993, "Three Strikes Law"(AB-971), co-authored by California Senators Wyman and Presley (an adoptive parent), would eventually affect Noah as it replaced *discretion* of the courts with statutory *"mandatory minimum sentences"* for *"repeat* offenders." Intended as a deterrent for *"violent* offenders," *non-violent* repeat offenders, like Noah, also got caught in the "Three Strikes" net:

> "If a Defendant has two or more prior convictions, the term for the current felony conviction shall be an indeterminate term of imprisonment in the state prison for life, with a minimum term of the indeterminate term as the greatest of (a) three times the term otherwise provided, as punishment for each current felony conviction subsequent to the two or more felony convictions, (b) imprisonment in the state prison for 25 years, or (c) the term determined by the court or the underlying conviction, including any applicable enhancement or punishment provisions."

And so on April 1, 1993, at age 34, Noah was back in prison when he wrote to my national adoption search and reform organization, Americans For Open Records (AmFOR). From his Arizona State Prison Complex SMU Unit, in Florence Arizona, he asked for assistance in finding his biological family:

> "Dear AmFOR, I got your address from the Salvation Army and there was only one sheet of information in the packet they sent me. I would like to hear more about your service. Yes, I am in prison here in Arizona but I am from Palm Desert, where my adoptive parents reside... Look, I know how some people think of people in prison, so I just want you to know I'm not a violent person. No guns and I didn't hurt anyone. Just an act of stupidity on my part. I had to say

this. I am an adopted person and I have been able to find out some information about my birth. I do know my birth name and a few other tidbits. I wrote to ALMA and others, but since I can't pay their fees, I get no help! If I could use a phone, it would help a lot, but all I have is writing. I get only so much done with this. I'm asking for help from you or someone and whether a fee is involved. I might be able to work something out. I get five cents an hour. Yes, five cents — for raking rocks. This is Arizona. Not much here but rocks. I really hope you or someone you know might be able to help me in my search. Thank you for your time. "

Although I had assisted many adoptees in their search for their biological families, free of charge, and had developed a national network of volunteers, each with their own approach to legally uncovering information and solving adoption puzzles without accessing "sealed" adoption records, Noah was the first of many *incarcerated* adoptees to contact me. His was the kind of search request that most adoption searchers generally *avoid*, both because prisoners cannot *pay* for search services and because searchers are leery of the prisoners' motives. Also, no one wanted to inform a birth parent that their child ended up behind bars. But Noah's subsequent letters, detailing parts of his life, alleging that his adoptive parents purchased him at a bar and later legalized his black market adoption, and that he had been abused as a child, was compelling, so I agreed to do what I could. Because I resided within a few blocks from his adoptive parents, Noah asked me to "look in on them" and to view his records that he was certain Gladys had kept.

The Gills lived in one of the 1960s small stucco homes, that still line Fairway Drive near the most exclusive Vintage Country Club homes of multi-millionaires. Then-elderly, White-haired, and frail, Herb and Gladys Gill, spent their days in front of their 25-inch console TV blaring loudly in their living room to compensate for their hearing loss. A feisty chain smoker with a perky bow atop her head, Gladys was not only hard of hearing but also slowly hobbled about with aid of her cane, yet was still able to pass a driving test with her glasses on. She wore a housecoat at home where the drapes were always drawn, cooling but also darkening the desert home throughout, except at the front window where Gladys watched for the mailman.

46

Official papers and letters related to Noah were kept throughout the house in neat piles where they had remained for many years – on the fireplace, in shoe boxes on the coffee table amid her cigarette packs and prescriptions, and on the floor at several spots all around the living room.

Gladys readily offered to provide me with whatever long forgotten details were in those piles, "in case it could help find his family. " She said she wanted her adopted son "to have relatives to go to, in case she and her husband are deceased by the time of his release from prison."

But rather than grant me unconditional access to whatever secrets the long guarded papers may reveal, Gladys doled them out, a few at a time, in exchange for favors – errands such as shopping for their groceries, prescriptions and Gladys' cigarettes, and loading Herb's wheelchair into the trunk of their big old Cadillac when taking them to their medical appointments, and to responding to Gladys's emergency calls to come over quickly to lift Herb up off the floor whenever he fell.

Some of Gladys' idiosyncrasies included watching a small battery operated TV on the front seat of her car with the windows rolled up so as "not to be distracted from a TV program by the sound of traffic *while driving.*"

The author, with Gladys Gill, then-80, and her cat, Trilby.

One day, Gladys called me over to bury her cat, "Trilby." Trilby was the same name she had given all her previous deceased cats. When I got there, Gladys was at her usual place on the sofa... and I'll never forget the cat, stiff as a statue from full rigor mortis, dead for three days before Gladys was ready to part with her pet. She wanted Trilby to be buried in their backyard. Unable to come up with a plastic container that was big enough to accommodate Trilby, I nevertheless proceeded to dig the hole, but each time I thought the job was done, the cat's stiffened legs still stretched upward *above ground*, so I kept digging the hardened earth with Gladys supervising, until I finally told Gladys to turn away as I unceremoniously shoved poor Trilby into the hole as forcefully as I could until the "proper burial" was achieved.

Gladys repeatedly showed me Noah's childhood photos and the collection of award ribbons he had won in swimming meets in his adolescent years. Frequently, she'd also bring out his "rap" sheets (police reports), or one of his many early psychological studies. Each was accompanied by her vivid, detailed memories of Noah's childhood, as if it was yesterday, despite that Gladys' immediate memory was failing and causing her to repeat many of the same stories over and over... and over again.

Gladys was a "night person." I wasn't. Nevertheless, she would often phone me close to midnight with something else she had remembered, in case it could help facilitate the search for Noah's birth family. Then one day she produced his amended birth certificate and, finally, she also "remembered" where she'd put his *adoption papers*. They bore Noah's true birth name—as well as the *names* of the parents he had been begging to know for 30 years but instead Gladys had taunted him with promises to tell him *"if he was good!"*

And so it evolved that in my desire to help an incarcerated adoptee discover his pre-adoption past, I also agreed to Gladys' request that I travel in place of Gladys and Herb to Noah's upcoming parole hearing, 300 miles away in the middle of the Arizona desert, in exchange for a few dollars for gas.

On Thursday, September 30, 1993, only five days before his parole hearing that was scheduled for the following Monday, October 4, I hit pay dirt in the search for Noah's biological mother.

Although Noah's mother never had a driver's license, the California Department of Motor Vehicles (DMV) had issued her an ID Card that

provided a cross-reference to her current married name, "Fernandez." Nowadays, DMV will not give out such information, but back then I was able to come up with not only her current name, but also her address.

However, she had no phone service. So, on a Friday in September, 1993, I sent her a telegram:

> "To Jacqueline Sue Treadwell Fernandez, in Duarte, California":
>
> "URGENT. PLEASE CALL ME COLLECT TODAY. YOUR SON KENNETH GENE OWENS (GILL) WOULD LOVE TO MEET YOU AND HIS SISTER THIS WEEK. (Signed) Lori Carangelo, AmFOR."

Meanwhile, I pressed Gladys for any "*good* memories" she had about her son, so that I might share then with his birth mother, Gladys replied:

> "*I don't remember any.*"

When I asked Gladys if she was *affectionate* toward him, and did she hold him when he was little, she was more certain:

> "When we first got him, he always wanted me to pick him up wherever we went... *and I thought this was odd.*"

> *"It is the nature of man to find people one is*
> *connected to by birth.*
> *The Italians have a saying:*
> *'Blood seeks blood.'"*
> --Lorraine Dusky, in "Birthmark"

9.
REUNION

Noah's biological sister, Susan, who was adopted separately, had already found their mother, Jackie Sue, with whom she was living. On Thursday, September 30, 1993, upon reading the telegram I had sent to Jackie, Susan immediately called me. After an emotional exchange, Susan could be heard through the telephone receiver at the other end calling out to her mother:

> *"It's KENNY...*
> *They found KENNY!..*
> *And he's in PRISON!"*

She then handed the phone to Jackie. Joyful, and at the same time tearful, in anticipation of the promised reunion with their son and brother at an Arizona prison, the two women had more hurdles to overcome. Jackie recently had her purse stolen and, with it, her DMV ID Card. It would be needed to permit her access to the prison and her son. But there was just one business day left on Friday in which to try to get Jackie and Susan "cleared" for a weekend visit before Noah's parole hearing on Monday, and to pick up both women in Duarte, bring them to my condo for an over-night stay, compare information on the missing years of Noah's life and how it was that Noah ended up with the Gills, glean whatever I could about *their* lives and then transport them to the high security prison in the middle of nowhere in the Arizona desert.

Jackie confirmed that Noah had two other siblings who had been adopted outright from the hospital when they were born— "Baby Boy Owens," in Bakersfield, and Diane Owens, in San Francisco. But Jackie didn't want anyone to find them, so would not provide a Waiver of Confidentiality to Social Services for disclosure, and would not explain why. The search for Noah's siblings would have to wait.

There was no way of directly contacting Noah ahead – so he was expecting to meet only me on Sunday, "Visitor's Day." The family reunion

51

- if it was going to take place - would be a total surprise to him.

Neither Jackie nor Susan had a car, and I didn't want to put miles on my pristine Camaro, so we three women piled into a rental car, bound for Florence, Arizona.

For hours after crossing the checkpoint at the California-Arizona border, we saw nothing but flat, open desert. And then, suddenly, the prison ominously loomed high on a hill before us - a fortress of stone and metal razor wire gleaming in the blazing desert sun. Parking was at the base of the hill that we had to climb while kicking desert sand out of our shoes. The first obstacles of just getting us there now behind us, I still hoped the prison officials would allow Jackie in, as I again explained the situation and showed them her alternate ID card.

We were in!

After a short wait in the Visitors' Room, Noah was brought in. Jackie and Susan were visibly shaken to see their now-adult son and brother for the first time since he was 3 – in chains. Noah and I exchanged greetings and I explained to him that I had brought "friends" along. If my words registered, he did not immediately look away from my eyes as I was then telling him:

> "The reason I was late is that I had to first travel to Duarte to
> pick up *your mother*..." I paused as I tilted my head toward
> Jackie… "*and your sister*," then tilting toward Susan.

I held my breath as Noah took a moment to digest this, still with his back to the two women he had been looking for most of his life. So I nodded a confirmation and he then turned to Jackie and Susan, his mouth falling open in silent utterance, as he suddenly buried his face in his hands, unaccustomed to showing his emotion. Then, suddenly, as if on cue, mother, sister and son were in a tearful huddled embrace, their muffled "I love you's" now drawing interest from other visitors and even an approving smile from the guard.

On Monday, October 4, 1993, the day after his emotion-charged reunion with his mother and sister at the Arizona prison, the CBS-TV (Phoenix Affiliate) camera man I hoped would be allowed in, filmed the hearing as the Arizona Parole Board listened to his family's pleas for his release. The proceedings were supported by my information with regard to "Adopted Child Syndrome" and how his unfortunate adoption placement impacted Noah's life.

The Board *granted* Noah his parole.

The CBS camera was still rolling when I made a statement in support of the pending Arizona "open records bill." I asked the camera man when it would be aired and he indicated "On tonight's 6:00 News" and that I could request a copy of the tape soon thereafter.

But the tape never made it to the Phoenix affiliate station for the evening broadcast — and no one could explain what happened to it -- one of those mysteries on often encountered in Adoption, particularly when a most politically powerful prison parole board is involved.

Jackie Sue and Noah

"It is very important to transcend the places that hold us."
-Rubin "Hurricane" Carter
from the movie, "Hurricane"

10.
REVOLVING DOOR OF THE 8 BALL CAFE

After his parole hearing in Florence, Noah was counting down the last few days remaining on his concurrent 15-year sentence where he had been transferred at Perryville, Arizona, for a theft that he had previously committed to buy drugs. He was then allowed to transfer his parole to California because I sponsored him and I was then closer to the California-Arizona border, a shorter drive than Florence had been, I picked him up on the day of his release.

I was living in a furnished 2-bedroom leased condo, and so offered to provide Noah a room from which he planned to turn his Indian beading hobby into a jewelry business. But also, for the first time, Noah would have the option of *not* returning to Gladys and hopefully have a better chance to successfully rehab. So, when I picked him up at Perryville, and he asked me to detour to the Phoenix Swap Meet "to buy beading supplies," it seemed a good idea. I had made a good living by supplementing my secretarial job income with profits from selling cars and furniture that I restored cosmetically, and could help him market and sell his handmade items to shops frequented by tourists. And so I also took him with samples of his handmade jewelry to Palm Springs, Idyllwild and Santa Barbara shops and crafts shows.

But, unknown to me, even before his release, Noah had already lined up drug suppliers in Arizona and California via an efficient prison grapevine. Boxes of beads he purchased when we stopped at the Phoenix Swap Meet, that were quickly slid into the lift-back of my Chevy Camaro, were transported along with Noah to California, I would later learn had been hiding marijuana and hard drugs, making Chevy Camaro a "drug mobile." If we had been stopped at the border for a random search, we both would have been arrested and my car would have been seized along with the drug,. I had a lot more to learn about Noah and addiction.

Photos of the author with Noah –
(Left): on the day of his release From Perryville Prison, and
(Right): trip to Santa Barbara for the arts and crafts show

Prior to Noah's release, Herb died. I was unaware, until Noah told me much later, that he had managed to transfer Gladys' and Herb's life savings of $45,000 to his own account. Gladys had put the account in the name that her husband and son shared — "*Herbert Gill*"— perhaps more to hide assets in anticipation of Herb's medical bills, than to help their son avoid complexities of probate. Apparently it never dawned on Gladys that her adopted son could easily assume ownership before both parents' demise. Or perhaps she thought that by having a will in which she left everything to *her nephew*, she would not be enabling Noah to buy drugs after her demise. But Noah said he felt Gladys "owed it to him." Besides, he reasoned, she wouldn't even *know* the savings account was cleaned out because she lived on her Social Security check that she cashed each month. His plan worked.

Noah, counting Gladys' cash.

He spent some of her money paid for his own Chevy Camaro, but most of it went to drug dealers. It wasn't long before it was apparent that Noah was "using" – at least smoking "pot. And when I drove Noah to the local parole office to keep his first appointment, the officer on duty referred to Noah as *"a career criminal."* Ever optimistic, I replied *"Anyone is potentially rehabilitatable."*

Almost immediately after Noah reported to the parole office, there was an unannounced visit from his parole officer, a nice young woman who confided that her brother had died from a heroin overdose, and who warned me that I "didn't know what I was getting into. Without letting on that I already suspected he was using drugs, as I still believed he could rehab if given a chance and if Gladys didn't resume her control of him or try to, I asked her about options for "relocating" Noah. There weren't any. Unless I could find him a new sponsor, and that was unlikely -- Jackie and Susan said they did not have an extra room for him -- Gladys' eagerness to house him, now that she was alone, was his only other option.

Noah wasn't with Gladys long before she phoned me calmly saying *"He's doing it again,"* indicating urgency in my going over to see what it was he was "doing again." When I arrived, Gladys just pointed to the bathroom. There, I found Noah standing in the shower, fully dressed, with knives at his throat, threatening to kill himself, high on "speed" and hallucinating that he was "seeing FBI men coming through the windows" and didn't want to go back to prison. Whether from intuition or lack common sense, I dropped to the floor to be lower than him and so perhaps less threatening, lest I be mistaken for an "FBI agent".... and just tried talking him down while Gladys phoned 911 as I had motioned for her to do. By the time the sheriff arrived, Noah had simply fallen asleep right there in the shower. The deputies had quietly snuck in and captured him. It was sad watching Noah being taken away on a stretcher in handcuffs and restraints, and knowing that the longest he could be detained at Riverside County General Hospital in Riverside "for 72-hour observation" – and then what? When it was time, I drove to Riverside and picked up Noah who was quiet on the ride back to Palm Desert except to say he *will* attempt suicide again. Nothing prepares a person to "say the right thing" in such a situation, because there is no "right thing" to say. I could only come up with what I hoped would penetrate his drugged brain but not in a way that sounded scolding as he was used to hearing from Gladys, and so in an unemotional, matter-of-fact soft tone, I ventured to reply:

"Okay, but if you kill yourself today,
you'll never know what tomorrow might have brought."

He seemed either surprised by my response or too tired to debate it and after a minute or so said,

"I'll think about that."

I no sooner dropped him off at Gladys' home that he hot the road to the high desert hippie community at Joshua Tree, just over the mountain from Palm Desert, where he said he was "living in a tent" and where it was "easy to connect with less expensive drug dealers."

Noah's next arrest highlighted an addict's disregard for the "law of probability" when he and any equally disheveled companion lifted the hood of a car in a shopping center parking lot in broad daylight and proceeded to steal the battery-- in full view of several people watching them through the glass front of a bank building a few feet away. He was sentenced under "Three Strikes Law" *to 15 years for theft of a car battery.*

During Noah's subsequent incarceration at California's "model" Substance Abuse Treatment Facility (CSATF) at notorious Corcoran State Prison, Noah used heroin for the first time. Drug dealers inside Corcoran extorted tens of thousands of dollars from Noah—money from the proceeds of his adoptive parents' home after Gladys died in January 1998, then valued at $120,00, but which he sold for $50,000 via a real state agent, to head off foreclosure

Noah wrote to me while he was at Corcoran:
"The guards refer to Corcoran's model drug rehab prison as 'sixty million dollars of waste.' You have to be a year away from going home to be in their drug program. There are seven yards, overcrowded with inmates, but only one drug program." At the time, the State of California was building four more "drug prisons." When Noah's life was threatened over drug bills he could no longer pay, he named names in exchange for protection via administrative segregation, which is solitary confinement. It was a year before he was moved to a "safe" yard at Mule Creek State Prison in Ione, California. How does one explain such dependence on drugs? Patti Davis, daughter of Ronald and Nancy

Reagan, herself an addict, summed it up in *"Dope: A Love Story"* (*"Viewpoint: America's Shadow Drug War,"* TIME, May 7, 2001, p 49):

"I never got arrested like Robert Downey Jr.—more because of dumb luck or chance than anything else. But if I had been arrested, my eyes would have looked the same as his—a hard, puzzling, far away stare into the camera. It isn't smugness. It's actually honesty. It's a look that says. There, now you know who I really am. I'm not lying and pretending I know how to live in this world. I don't. Not alone, not without my lover. Remember how Robert Downey Jr. described his relationship with drugs at his hearings? He said *'It was like I had a gun in my mouth, and I loved the taste of the gun-metal.'* You will never understand drug addiction unless you understand that it's a *love story*." Drug addiction is only a by-product of Noah Stone's root problem—the failed experiment called adoption.

Four decades of analytical and anecdotal documentation had been amassed on Noah Stone by helping professionals, hospitals, police, agencies, courts and prisons. For years prior to his first incarceration, the documentation often mentioned his adoptive status, his unsuitable adoptive parents, his longing to connect with his birth family, and his drug addiction. Yet he was provided no adoption-oriented support, no family contact, no adoption or addiction oriented therapy, no daily living skills, no marketable job skills training, nor education, while institutionalized.

Throughout his formative years, Noah was abused physically, probably sexually, certainly emotionally, and with prescription drugs from those entrusted with his care, education and counseling. He was introduced to heroin at California's "model" Substance Abuse Treatment Facility (CSATF) at Corcoran State Prison and for most of his life, Noah resided in prison cells, supposedly monitored, occasionally taking up a hobby craft, but mostly bored and just waiting for the days, weeks, months and years to pass before his next parole date. He had no prospects for any other life and so the system repeatedly reclaimed him. Birth bonds, reunions, reconciliation and adoption healing, alone, do not necessarily change a life. For Noah and other lifelong addicts, resurrection will require decriminalization of drugs and appropriate long term treatment, rather than incarceration, as actor Robert Downey Jr. received for his drug addiction under California' sentencing law.

Their birth bond led him to his other his other sister--and to the fact that his brother who he always sensed existed, despite others' denials, *does* exist. But the bond between Noah and his mother, who was battling addictions of her own, led Noah back to drugs and self destructive behaviors. I had rushed him to hospital emergency rooms whenever he overdosed.

When Noah held knives at his throat threatening suicide while high on "speed," the sheriff would apprehend him, but after the maximum "72-hour Observation and Detox," Noah would head back to his drug dealer.

At a faith-based, 12-step "Narcotics Anonymous" meeting for friends and relatives of addicts, I was told that Noah would have to "hit bottom" before he could turn his life around. For Noah, hitting "bottom" would most certainly be *fatal*. On March 11, 2011, Noah wrote:

> "Since the last time I saw you I've done some very bad things to myself and I'm worse than I've ever been. The 'meth' I did put *'holes' in my brain* and there are voices in those holes that I can hear. They say things that make me mad and sad. But being sad in my life is something I'm very used to. I'm so tired. There's no way I can explain how tired I have become with my life and the things I've done to other people. I feel sad that I stole people's treasures from them that they can never get back. God is very mad at me. I know this because my voices tell me so. I won't hurt myself or others anymore, so that God will be happy with me and will tell the voices to stop and so he'll fix the holes so the voices will go away. I want to be happy again. I remember when you got me out of Arizona State Prison. That was a very good time. I felt that I was myself for awhile. What have I become since? I've left nothing to the world, nothing to make anything better for anyone, no kids. After me, there is nothing."

Noah enclosed a poem he wrote, titled *"All My Gone Years"*:

"All the gone years I have seen.
All the things that could have been.
My life before me, I took away in a single shot in a single day.
May brain has holes with voices that say
'Your life is nothing but decay.'
In my mind's eye, I see a happier time,
when summer days would go slowly by.
But first there came a mother who put me in a very dark space.
Stairs are for climbing, not throwing down.
Why did she laugh when I hit the ground?
I can't stomach the food she made me eat
but if I refused she made me bleed.
In my dark place, I hear my voices say,
'Run now...There'll be better days.'
But they brought me back to her,
back to her hands that went Whack!
And I felt that bone crack!
All the gone years I have left behind.
Just the voices inside my holes.
I've lost my mind.
Should I live or should I die?
The next shot will decide.
All my gone years are now inside the holes."

He also wrote that he has Stage 2 Hepatitis C, his lungs hurt, and he had been on anti-seizure and anti-anxiety medication but asked the prison doctor to "stop his medication for the voices" because he doesn't like that drug. I haven't heard from him since. Prison had been Noah's safest "home" with fewer torments, but he no longer shows up on California's inmate locator website nor anywhere else. Having no place to live, or die, undoubtedly Noah was ready to "go home."

> *"There are only six degrees of separation*
> *between me and everyone else on the planet.*
> *But oh to find the right six."*
> –from "Six Degrees of Separation,"
> by John Guare

EPILOGUE

The Biblical Noah's genealogy is recorded in the Book of Genesis as result of saving his son's and his sons' wives so the human species could survive—the first experiment in **"eugenics"**-- *genetic* breeding. Unlike the genealogy of Biblical Noah, Noah Stone's family tree is a pile of broken branches—a testament to the failure of **"euthenics,"** controlling a species through *environmental* factors resulting in *learned* behaviors.

Noah's Maternal Family Tree:

- Ancestors from Waleetka, Oklahoma, include Grandpa John Treadwell's mother who was full-blooded Native American of the Blackfoot tribe.

- Noah's mother, Jackie Sue Treadwell Owens, was devastated by the loss of her 4 children, including Kenneth, aka Noah, who were **adopted** out when she was only 17; Jackie then battled a lifelong addiction to alcohol. Jackie Sue's brother, Harmon Dale Treadwell, married Margaret Attaway and **adopted** Russell, Margaret's child by her prior marriage.

- Jackie Sue's sister, Lillian, **adopted** Robert Friar.

- Emerald Eugene Friar **adopted** out one child and then **adopted** Mike Friar.

- Charlene Davis **adopted** out one son.

- Helen Foshee remarried and had one son who was later **adopted** by Billie Foshee.

- Uncle John Henry aka "The Bandit" spent time in *prison*.

- Janet Marie Friar, Marion Edward Friar, and his wife Jan, all committed **suicide.**

Most of Noah's life had been driven by his need to know his past and the need to dull his pain with drugs. Noah's other sister, Melody, had been found. and his brother, Robert, who was a long-distance delivery driver with many forwarding addresses, was being tracked down. Melody, a soft-spoken religious woman, said she had "a wonderful life with wonderful adoptive parents" and she planned to be supportive to her new-found brother, Noah.

PART 2:

TOM McGEE

Mugshot – Young Tom McGee

"Hope is that thing with feathers,
that perches in the soul
and sings the tune without the words
and never stops at all."
-Emily Dickinson

1.
CONNECTING

Like most adoptee, Thomas Kent McGee had always wanted to know who his mother was. Not just know her name, but see and know *her*. But as in most states, his pre-adoption birth records were sealed by a court and he didn't know how to even begin an inquiry.

Then one day Tom found a listing for AmFOR that helped adult adoptees to locate their biological families. without charge. That's when Tom set into motion and active search for his mother, as he began to write a brief letter mailed from the Mental Health Section of California State Prison at Vacaville, California to my organization, Americans For Open Records (AmFOR). His letter was acknowledged with my request for any further known adoption information, to which he immediately responded.

At this point, I will let Tom tell his own story as he detailed it in his letters.

April 19, 1999: "Dear Lori, Your reply letter is truly a blessing--one I have prayed for since I was told I am adopted. It warms my heart just to find someone so committed to taking the mystery out of the lives of those in the adoption triad. I found Americans For Open Records listed in a book on our prison library bookshelves called *'Search'* by Jayne Askin. Jayne herself is an adoptee.

Basically, I want to know about my past -- where I came from. As an adoptee, I sometimes feel like I was *just dropped here from outer space*. What are my roots? Do I have brothers and sisters? I do wish to establish contact. My main fear, however, is my mother's reaction to my incarceration. Will she be disappointed that her son is a drug addict in prison? I am prepared to deal with knowing her situation, no matter what it may be. Not knowing at all is worse than knowing, even if knowing may hurt. I sincerely hope she feels the same way.

I have been saying 'she,' referring only to my mother, but I have the same interest in my father and possible siblings.

In the past, people have discouraged me from searching. I've been told of the difficulties and enormous cost. When I contacted Fresno County Social Services, they further discouraged me by citing "privacy laws." Also, having been incarcerated in one way or another more than half my life, my resources are very limited. I did register at no cost with International Soundex Reunion Registry (ISRR). I also filed my Consent For Contact with Fresno County Social Services.

I was born June 24, 1975, in Fresno, California. I was informed that, at some time before I was six months old, my mother considered giving me up and when I was six months old, Fresno County Social Services made the decision for her and placed me in foster care. And that is where I remained for 5 years until approximately May 1980.

I'm not sure what date my adoption was finalized, but I know I was placed with the McGees about a month before my 5th birthday. I've seen my *Amended* Birth Certificate but no longer have a copy.

It was over ten years after my adoptive parents' request for more information about me, when I was in my teens, before Fresno Social Services would release just '*non-identifying* background information' about me. It revealed that my background is Mexican, Japanese and Caucasian. It also mentioned that my mother had been diagnosed with and treated for Paranoid Schizophrenia. She was described as an "*addict and alcoholic,*" as was my father. She also served time in Youth Authority for reasons not indicated. So I wrote to the Director of Department of the Youth Authority in Sacramento for information on my mother and her last known known address. This is the reply:

> "September 30, 1993: Dear Thomas: You state that you are an adoptee and are requesting that our department assist you in finding your biological mother. You describe that your biological mother was committed to the Youth Authority at age 14, from Merced County. By law, our department cannot release any information on persons who were committed to us as

a juvenile. There are other avenues that you can pursue in your search. You might want to contact private groups that specialize in this, such as the Adoptees Liberty Movement Association (ALMA), which can be found in most larger cities' yellow pages. You can also pursue public records such as the county hall of records for birth information, federal Social Security System, hospital records, etc.

Sincerely, Francisco J. Alcorn, for William B. Kolender, Director; cc: Greg Zermo, Supt. Preston School; Scott Pierce, SPA, Oakland Parole."

Alcorn seemed to be trying to help Tom, but he apparently didn't know that ALMA would have charged $65 per year just to list Tom on its passive registry "in case" someday his mother might learn of their registry and pay $65 also. As for Alcorn's suggestion about pursuing public records for birth information, he must have forgotten that adoptees don't know their biological parents' names, nor their own birth name -- In California, as in most states, those names are "sealed" in the court file. Tom was clearly telling the officials what he needed, but it seemed to him that no one was listening.

Tom's letter continued: "I can't possibly adequately express my gratitude for your detailed personal response. You've given me some hope that I may finally be able to feel that I *belong*... and hope has eluded me for quite some time. I understand there are no guarantees, but hope is good. Hope is really good.

As for the rest of my background information, I was told that my father attempted suicide shortly after my birth, and that my mother neglected my nutritional needs during the six months I was with her... and that she gave up my older half-brother for adoption but kept my other brother. I was also told that my family lived in Merced and Fresno and that I was in many foster homes. My *adoptive* parents have one biological daughter about eleven years older than me. She manages a store that her husband owns, she's a real estate agent, and attends college part-time to study architecture. She has never had any problems with drugs, alcohol or the law. She is supportive and a sociable person. My adoptive dad is Irish. He's a train operator and owns and operates a small business. He served in the military and never has any problems with drugs, alcohol or the law. He is supportive but cannot understand my many problems. He is understandably frustrated and is close to giving up on me. Several times, he was offered the opportunity to *nullify* my adoption but chose not to. My adoptive mom was born and raised in Japan and adheres to traditional Japanese values. She is a data entry clerk for Contra Costa County and also assists my father in their store. She has been supportive *at a distance*. I think she *has* given up on me.

My adoptive parents said they adopted me because they wanted a second child and also wanted to give a 'disadvantaged child' an opportunity. They specifically requested an older child of mixed race.

I now have hope of eventually finding my family. Anything you can do to assist me will be greatly appreciated. "

"Don't do the crime
if you can't do the time."
-Robert Blake, actor,
in "Baretta," ABC TV series (1975-1978)

2.
CRIME and PUNISHMENT

According to Tom:

"By age 5, I was already having many problems. I was suspended from kindergarten for fighting. My behaviors indicated mental problems. For some unknown reason, whenever I heard a police or ambulance siren, I would make a violent effort to get out of wherever I was. I grew out of it but there was never an explanation.

At age 10 or so, I committed arson. I started a grass fire on a hill next to my elementary school and convinced the fire department it was an accident, so I was never charged. By this time my IQ test indicated I was far above average, yet my grades were mostly D's and F's.

When I was about 12, a friend and I got caught stealing beef jerky strips from a store in the mall. The judge ordered probation and a treatment program. By this time I was already drinking a beer every day. One day I took my beer to school. I thought it was cool. A kid told on me and I was locked up in Juvenile Hall for the first time. I started a couple of programs but kept running away and began experimenting with drugs.

During my 12th year, I committed two residential burglaries stealing things of little or no monetary value. In fact, I burglarized one home numerous times and was finally caught inside the home but no charges were filed. I also burglarized another home, a small fruit stand, and even a fire department, but I was never caught and so no charges were filed.

At age 13, a neighbor introduced me to marijuana, and in my freshman year I experimented with LSD, codeine, and speed. The only thing I looked forward to was getting high. Nothing else mattered.

I was finally arrested for possessing alcohol and a switchblade knife on a school campus and found myself in Juvenile Hall which I immediately tried to escape. I rang my buzzer around midnight to use the restroom knowing only two staff members were working then. On the way back to my cell, unguarded, I grabbed the fire extinguisher. When a guard came back to lock me in, I bolted out of my cell with the fire extinguisher, spraying him in the face, and tried to hit him with the canister. He tackled me and busted my chin. I had to go to the hospital to get three stitches. It was the first time I had done anything that could be considered 'violent.' I felt it was self defense. I just wanted to be free. While awaiting placement at Bear Creek Ranch prior to my first lockup at Juvenile Hall, I had been dinking alcohol and experimented with marijuana.

Over the next seven years, I was in several residential facilities -- Bear Creek Ranch, Full Circle, Family Life Center, Our Family, Oakendell, and Rite of Passage. The one called "Our Family" was a drug treatment program. I was also in three different juvenile halls -- in Napa, Solano and Sonoma countries. During those seven years, I spent less than one year on the street -- sometimes as little as thirty days at a time.

At age 19, while in California Youth Authority (CYA), I joined Norte XIV, a gang of Hispanics from Northern California that has a presence in California prisons. But I decided I didn't really *belong*, so I stopped 'banging' and became a Christian, as religion is the only 'honorable' way out of a prison gang. But upon being transferred to another facility, I started banging again and quit again.

Upon parole from CYA, I met some other Nortenos who were in their teens and we ran together while I was staying with Pam, a woman five years my senior and who was married with four kids. She left her husband and I moved in with her and quit my job. She got pregnant with my first child, her fifth child.

I kept using drugs -- mostly methamphetamine -- and worked odd jobs erratically for about a year until we broke up. When she left me, I attempted suicide and ended up in a hospital under 72-hour observation. Upon release from the hospital, I went home to my adoptive parents and got a job at a fast food restaurant. Within thirty days, my adoptive dad kicked me out for using drugs.

For the next six months, I lived under bridges, committed a gang-related assault, and was sentenced to prison. I was banging in San Quentin and in Folsom for about a year. The judge gave me a six year sentence but offered to suspend it if I would enter a two-year drug program. I took the program. But 45 days later, I left the program by stealing a van and was arrested the same day for Auto Theft and Driving Under the Influence (DUI). My total prison term was eight years.

I again tried Christianity but didn't *fit* in there either. Because I had a cellie who was a Muslim, even though most prison Muslims are Black, they accepted me and I studied the religion with determination. I'm now a Muslim. One of our Muslim traditions is to grow facial hair. I've been growing a beard for the past year and now CDC has a new policy prohibiting beards. They make no exceptions for religion. Most of the Muslims complied and shaved. Still wanting to be accepted, I *kept* my beard. That's what earned me my 'C' status or program failure, and I may have to serve a year and a half more in prison unless I shave. But, you know, I still don't feel like I *fit in*. I guess there is no substitute for knowing who you are and where you came from.

My drug history includes alcohol, marijuana, LSD, mushrooms, opium, methamphetamine and heroin. On the streets. when I worked, I spent my paycheck on drugs. Occasionally I sold drugs or transported drugs to earn a cut to support my habit. I even engaged in homosexual activity in desperation to obtain drugs.

I am currently drug-free."

A Youth Authority Report on Thomas Kent McGee, #YA67351, lists his Offense History through 1993, including attempted Petty Theft, Minor and Major Drinking in Public, Possession of a Switchblade Knife, Escape (walk away) from Juvenile Hall, Battery on a Custodial Officer, Fighting in Public, and Battery." The report detailed Tom's social history. Under "Self Perceptions" it was noted:

> "The ward further states 'A lot of my problems are based on my natural mother's decision to put me up for adoption. I also have a lot of problems centered on drugs. Drugs used to be a big problem for me. They aren't anymore.

73

Overall, I'm a pretty likable guy. I've got my bad points like everyone but my positive qualities outweigh the negative ones.'"

And under "Clinical Impressions":

"At no time during any interview together did this young man present evidence of psychosis or other major thought disorders, Additionally, there was no evidence of suicidal ideation or intent either in the past or present. It is clear that Thomas McGee is an exceptionally intelligent young man. His academic skills and ability to communicate far surpass most every CYA ward which this caseworker has interviewed. Unfortunately, for various reasons, Thomas has not capitalized on his intelligence and other positive qualities. Thomas appears to be the product of an intact and stable environment from his adoptive parents. However, he seems alienated from his family and has turned to his peers for a sense of belonging. Clinical impressions of this young man suggest that he is manipulative, impulsive and without insight. There also appears to be hostility and anger toward his adoptive parents and those in authority. He presented as mature and cooperative, but he is superficial in his relationships with adults. At this time, it is recommended that parole be Denied and he be placed in an appropriate CYA facility where his treatment and management needs can best be addressed."

3.
FAKING CRAZY

"As for my psychiatric history, the many diagnoses I received have been inaccurate because I hide some symptoms and fake others. I saw a psychologist regularly from age 15 to 18. In prison, I sought psychiatric care primarily to obtain medications -- legal drugs. After awhile, I finally admitted to myself that I really do have problems.

If the psychiatrist "thinks you're crazy enough" he can upgrade your status to Enhanced Outpatient Program (EOP), which offers a minimum of 10 hours of therapy/counseling per week as opposed to the usual one hour every 90 days. Upon obtaining EOP status, I transferred to the Department of Mental Health Section of the California Department of Corrections. I'm in a better place now. I feel safe here and I'm feeling better.

I've never communicated with a mother who had lost a child to adoption before. Your enthusiasm and dedication to this cause is commendable. And I really appreciate your assistance. I've obtained a copy of my Amended Birth Certificate. My adoptive parents thank you for helping me with letters and such.

I am told that the circumstances leading to my adoption were that my birth parents were young, unemployed and had medical, psychiatric and legal problems. Even so, the family situation may have improved with help. Even if it didn't, they and I have a right to know each other and whether we are alive and well.

As for my *adoptive* parents, my adoptive father used to use his belt to discipline me, and once pointed his hunting rifle at me at our camp in Modoc. We'd had an argument and I said I was leaving. I got about a quarter mile away when I heard him about a hundred yards behind me. When I turned around, I saw him kneeling on the ground pointing his 30/30 rifle at me and ordering me to come back. As soon as I started back, he got up and walked back to camp ahead of me. We never talked about it. Maybe we should have. And maybe I should talk to Mom too.

I fantasize about things related to *power and control.* In one fantasy, I have a private prison of my own where I take people off the street and lock them up. I have always had a small burn mark, about three inches long, on my right leg -- the width of perhaps a curling iron or something like that. I can't explain it and have no memory of how or when it happened. I also have cigarette burns all over my left arm and a few other places but I know *those* are *self-inflicted.* It's how I used to deal with stress. The freshest burns are from this year.

I daydream about sex, probably excessively. This is difficult to talk about because I have, as recently as this year, engaged in homosexual acts to obtain drugs. I don't like it, but I did it, and I'm disgusted with myself for it. Other than that, I guess everything is normal. I lost my virginity at age 19 when I paroled from CYA -- four sexual partners in 18 months -- one for a year, one for 30 days, one for 2 weeks, and a one-nighter.

My waking hours are spent in a dreamlike state. When I apply myself, I excel. When I get bored, I get stubborn and under-achieve. In elementary school, my IQ scores were high, yet my grades were low. In prison, my academic scores were off the chart, yet I always end up in trouble and can't hold a job. I ran away from home and seven other places. My first conflict with authority was when I was suspended from kindergarten. I usually only lie to avoid getting into trouble, not for amusement or premeditated deception.

I mentioned the arson. Most of the time I stole for the thrill of it. It was like a game and I felt like I was winning, the prize being that I kept what I stole even though it was of little or no value. Perhaps it had something to do with the power."

Tom had enumerated all eight Adopted Child Syndrome behaviors.

"Perhaps the most important thing
we ever give each other
is our attention."
-Rachel Naomi Remen

4.
MORE BENEFITS OF BEING CRAZY

In his letter dated May 25, 1999, Tom felt he needed to explain further:

"At first, I tried being 100% honest with the psychiatric staff. But they decided I 'wasn't crazy enough' to take the time to help me. So I studied the *Diagnostic and Statistical Manual of Mental Disorders* and decided on 'schizo-effective' because inmates who seem to be 'crazy' get better treatment. They have better access to counseling and more services upon parole. They are immediately eligible for disability insurance. I now get the highest level of treatment available.

I'm not crazy, but sometimes you have to be crazy to get their attention. Make sense? I didn't want to put this on paper because a nurse will read this and they'll know I'm manipulating them and the system... but I want to be straightforward with you.

I have a lot of anxiety when around others. I always feel "off," like I *don't belong.* I feel that others are laughing at me and making fun of me. I'm insecure. But compared to other men in prison, I believe I have strong morals. I try not to use profanity, unless to make a point. When I was homeless, I no longer stole - not even to provide myself with food - as I felt sincere remorse for my childhood stealing and will never do any more burglaries. I also would never hit a woman or a child. I've been respectful of the prison guards and don't hate then - I hate the system. The guards are just doing their jobs, trying to fed their families.

Overall, I'm a good guy. But I have some *identity* problems. In many ways, I'm still the 12-year old kid who got locked up so young. I've never been able to decide *who I am.* I know that if I find my biological family, then I'll know I *really exist* and have a true origin... that I came from Mr. and Mrs. so-and-so. Knowing where I came from and who I am can help me decide where I'm going and who I want to be.

My current medications include Prozac and Olanzapine.

I'm not very sociable. Never had many friends. The way I met my ex-girlfriend, the mother of my child, was a fluke, as I'll explain..."

5.
FATHERHOOD and ADDICTION

"I was 19 and on parole from California Youth Authority (CYA) and selling Kirby vacuum cleaners door-to-door when I knocked on her door. She was 24, married with four kids. We got together, kicked her husband out, and I moved in against my adoptive parents' advice. We quit our regular jobs since she was also Manager of the apartment complex where we lived, and I became Assistant Manager.

Many of our tenants were "tweakers" (meth users) and I got hooked. I couldn't get enough of it. I still also drank and smoked pot, even dropped acid, and took mushrooms occasionally, but my drug of choice was "crank"- methamphetamine. Before long, she left me, taking our three-month old daughter with her.

That's when I made a failed suicide attempt.

After my suicide attempt, I returned to my adoptive parents' home again and got a job at Taco Bell, but lost the job in two weeks for smoking weed at work. Dad then kicked me out and I was homeless until I was locked up again.

I haven't seen my ex-girlfriend or daughter since.

At age 20, when I came to prison, I discovered I could get drugs just as easily as on the street... It was just more expensive. I smoked weed occasionally and used crack when it came my way. A couple of times, I drank some pruno - a prison wine, that is an alcoholic beverage variously made from apples, oranges, fruit cocktail, candy, ketchup, sugar, milk, and possibly other ingredients, including crumbled bread. Bread supposedly provides the yeast for the pruno to ferment.

But it was later at Folsom that I first snorted heroin. Heroin appealed to me because I felt a temporary crack-like rush before my body would settle into a comfortable heroin-induced stupor. While I was high, nothing else mattered. Everything was okay. I could forget, temporarily, that I was a dope fiend in prison. Before that, I never used a needle but was told that to really experience heroin, it had to be mainlined. I would justify smoking pot by saying 'Hey, at least I ain't hooked on heroin.'

I still smoke weed at least once a week and use heroin once a month or so. I also use psychotropic medications to get high. When I really want to feel flooded, I take a seizure pill (a barbiturate). Do I want to quit using drugs? At this moment, honestly, no, I don't. I want to use drugs, but I don't want to deal with the consequences. I want to feel in *control* of my drugs, but that can never happen because an addict can never control his drug use.

"In order to learn the most important lessons in life,
one must each day surmount a fear."
-Wayne Dyer

6.
ANGER

"Specific *triggers* to my anger include when I'm told what to do by someone I feel had no right to do so, and when others try to take my rights away, or when I'm questioned about my daily affairs. It could be as simple as being asked what I'm reading. What business is it of theirs? I get angry when I'm criticized or stereotyped, and when I don't meet my own expectations for myself - when I try and fail. I get angry when someone is inconsiderate of me and my emotions, or discount my ideas or opinions. I get angry when people challenge my intellect. And when I have to do someone else's job.

I even get angry about getting angry.

Anger, for me, stems from *fear...* fear that I might lose control over a situation. When I perceive that I have no *control,* I feel afraid and then become angry. It is often regarded as a masculine trait to be in control, so loss of control also challenges my self image of masculinity.

I deal with anger in several ways. Often, I just avoid the situation. If the situation can't be avoided, I *suppress* my feelings about it by imagining the worst possible outcome and then resign myself to accept it as inevitable, which removes the uncertainty. This 'knowledge' overcomes my fear and anger becomes unnecessary.

Another way I deal with anger is by aggressive action. If I can convince myself that I'm regaining *control* and asserting my masculinity through aggression, the outcome is irrelevant to me. Even if I don't regain control in the process, at least I made an effort and acted 'as a man should.'

I'm afraid that prison is going to change me even more than it has. Many guys in here are hardened and would just as soon kill you as shake your hand. I don't want to be like that. I want a life. I want to belong in society.

I want to be *normal.*

At the same time, I'm afraid to leave prison.

My adoptive parents have already let me know that they can't help me when I get out. I think my anxiety could turn into panic as my parole date approaches.

7.
HOMELESSNESS, DRUGS, AND A KIND OF THERAPY

When my adoptive Dad kicked me out for smoking and selling pot, and losing my job at Taco Bell, I spent the first night at a friend's house. The next day, I returned home while my adoptive parents were at work to steal some supplies - blankets, sleeping bags, pots, a knife, and a few other items.

My first night out in Vacaville, I met a group of 15 other homeless people who called themselves "The Crew." They taught me about collecting aluminum cans and glass to turn in as recyclables for cash. They also bought me alcohol as I was just under 21. I slept under a bridge, separate from theirs. Bridges would be necessary shelter as the winter rainy season was starting. But I preferred seclusion to sleeping at a group campsite.

I went into one shelter for about a week and they kicked me out for drinking, so I went back to my bridge and found The Crew waiting for me. One of them accused me of stealing one of their recycling routes, beat me senseless, and took all my money - about $10. Another guy in The Crew pulled a knife and threatened to kill me, but someone pulled him off me. I left with my tail between my legs and bleeding all over myself. I split up blood for two weeks after that.

In fear of my life, I moved to Fairfield where I found a new bridge - a Highway 80 overpass. No one was there so I made camp. A few days later, I met a guy who lived on the other side of the bridge. He invited me over and said I could use his stove if I bought the gas. I bought a can and moved over. He cooked every day, which was nice.

While there, I would occasionally go to my adoptive parents' store and ask for food, money and cigarettes. Dad said I could come home whenever I decided to quit using drugs, which was impossible for me at the time. I went back to the bridge. Being homeless was no fun, but I appreciate the experience.

In prison, my social worker and psychiatrist are aware that I'm an adoptee. But they seem oblivious to the problems that are unique to adoptees and to my particular situation. I rarely have any serious one-on-one sessions in which I can discuss it at all.

Doing time is easier for me as a single man than for guys who have families, wives, or girlfriends out there waiting for them. I've never had a wife or even a girlfriend for long, and have never been close with my adoptive family. I miss my freedom, but not that much, considering the last place I lived was under a bridge. So doing time is easier for me. Not *easy*, just *easier*.

I've never written this much to anyone. It's good for me because I'm releasing feelings and emotions that have been stored for too long. Writing to you has been therapy for me. It gives me an opportunity to release my past and validate my own existence. I am somebody. I don't have to be a dope fiend all my life. Perhaps if Fresno County Social Services had told me some of my *real* parents *good* qualities as well, I might not feel so *pre-destined* to be an addict. I know I don't want my daughter to be living an addict's life under a bridge."

June 27, 1999: "I'm close to making a final decision to quit drugs. I haven't had any pot since April, no heroin since March, no wine since December. I'm tired of the way drugs ruin my life. I could do so much better, but I need to figure out *what* to do and *how* to do it. Mostly I want to have a normal family."

The psychotropic drug group known as phenothiazines, specifically Mellaril (thioridazine) and Thorazine (chlorpromazine), that were being prescribed to Tom at this time, have serious side effects, including:

- sedation,
- urinary retention,
- dry mouth,
- constipation,
- blurred vision,
- cardiac arrhythmia,
- low blood pressure,
- dizzyness.

These drugs may also cause motor disorders similar to Parkinsons but this effect is reversible upon discontinuance of the drug. Overdose of Mellaril, however, may produce not only the same side effects but also convulsions and coma. Tom was also being given Prozac which can cause the following side effects:

- insomnia,
- vivid and violent dreams,
- absence of emotions,
- inability to feel guilt or to cry,
- nausea,
- rash,
- breathing or lung problems,
- cardiac palpitations,
- jitteriness,
- unusual energy surges (adrenaline rushes) producing super human strength,
- memory impairment,
- hair loss,
- blurred vision or pressure behind the eyes,
- cravings for alcohol, sweets and caffeinated drinks
- headaches,
- swelling and/or pain in the joints,
- muscle twitching or contractions,
- tongue numbness and slurred speech,
- sweating, chills or cold sweats,
- dizzyness,
- confusion,
- muscle weakness,
- muscle tremors or lack of coordination,
- extreme fatigue,
- diabetes or hypoglycemia,
- lowered immune system,
- seizures or convulsions,
- mood swings,
- altered personality,
- manic-like symptoms (i.e. restlessness, racing thoughts, hostility,
- deceitfulness,
- blank staring,

- hyperactivity,
- aggressive or violent behavior,
- impulsive behavior without concern for consequences,
- numbness in various body parts,
- isolating one's self,
- aversion to being touched,
- paranoia,
- feeling "possessed,"
- self-destructive behavior and suicidal attempts,
- mania, psychosis -- all the things for which inmates like Tom are treated to prevent.

"Ain't no mountain high enough
Ain't no valley low enough
Ain't no river wide enough
To keep me from getting to you..."
--Sung by Marvin Gaye 1976, Diana Ross 1970

8.
ONE SEARCH ENDS,
ANOTHER BEGINS

[Author's note: On July 29, 1999, an Americans For Open Records "informant" - an adoptive mother who owns California birth indexes - provided Tom McGee's birth name, his mother's maiden name, but not her first name, and his father's first and last name and middle initial. The informant usually charged $200 per name but shared Tom's identifying information because she will not deal with prisoners directly, and knows most are indigent and trusts my judgment in handling potential contacts made in this way.]

Tom's two notarized "Consent For Contact" forms and cover letter were mailed to Barbara Edmonston, Supervisor, Fresno County Social Services Adoption Division, by Certified Return Receipt Mail. Before mailing the forms, I added the surnames of Tom's biological mother, "Oka," and his father, "Ralls." My cover letter explained that any information that Edmonston could provide to Tom would assist his treatment and rehabilitation and, since a search for his biological parents was underway, it would be helpful to all parties to have some background information. Edmonston said they had been taking about six months to reply to requests for post-adoption information *"because they are not a priority."*

At the same time, I sent a letter to Tom, informing him that his birth name is "Thomas Ralls Jr.," that his mother's maiden name is "Oka," and that his father is "Thomas W. Ralls, Sr," and that I had checked for birth notices on microfilm of the 1975 editions of the Fresno Bee newspapers but I did not find any of the newly discovered names. Also, despite that Tom's birth certificate states he was born at Valley Medical Center, now called Community Health Systems, they still denied having any record of Tom's birth. Tom was excited to finally know his parents' names.

October 21, 1999 from Tom: "I received a letter from my adoptive parents. They have decided to give me one more chance. She enclosed a money order and said they will send a food package soon. I'm glad they are on my side. I will need their support when I get out. Perhaps they will be able to help me get a job where he works. At least I may have more options now."

On December 30, 1999, Tom's search for this mother was coming to an end when he wrote: "My family has found me! My mother is Cynthia Oka Perrett, and my father is Thomas Wayne Ralls Jr., just as you told me. I have one full brother, Ralphael Ralls, age 23, and three half-brothers - Jose, 28, Robert, 19, Russell, 9, and two half-sisters, Nikki, 20, and Victoria, 16. Nikki and Jose had hired a searcher and have been searching for me at the same time that we have been searching for them! They first located my adoptive parents. My Dad phoned the prison and left a message for me to call him. Robert is in Jail and they are still looking for Ralphael.

But my mother, Cynthia, is *dying of cancer. She has only about a month to live.*

Their address and phone number are enclosed. I'm so excited to finally have contact with my blood family. I still consider my adoptive parents my family also, as they have taken care of me and loved me all these years. They may not be very affectionate, and we don't talk much about our feelings, but they did finally give me my mother's contact information because she is dying. It's too bad I'm in prison and can't help take care of my mother as I would like to. I still believe Fresno County made some grave mistakes in dealing with my adoption case, but it doesn't seem important anymore. I am more concerned with finding out who everyone is and what their lives are like. I have so many questions.

Thank you for all your assistance and continuing efforts to now find my father. I know how hard it is when doors are closed. My earliest release date is now January 29, 2002 - only a year to go."

Although Tom tried asking the Warden for a temporary, supervised visit to see his mother for the first time before she dies, at the same time, I phoned Tom's family -- only to learn from his mother's sister, Christine, that Tom's mother died, December 30, 1999 - the day he wrote me that his family had found him.

Tom's mother died *knowing that Tom had been found*, but Tom would never get to see her. Christine was very sympathetic of Tom's situation and of adoptees' plight in general. She shared that during the few days between learning about Tom, and her sister's death, Tom's siblings also had begged the Warden to allow Tom just one brief visit, even under guard, so he could satisfy *her* last wish to see her son before she dies, and so he could be with the mother he never knew, but although Tom posed no danger to anyone, prison officials took no action toward that possibility. Now it was too late.

I notified Tom's prison counselor about his mother's passing and that I would locate his father. She agreed to deliver that message to Tom.

The irony is that Tom's mother and siblings had previously attempted to contact Tom through Merced County Social Services but were denied and simply told "records are sealed" but Merced did not direct the family to Fresno County Social Services, nor did they advise them that, under California law at the time, they could have filed a Waiver of Confidentiality and a Consent for Contact form with the branch that held Tom's adoption file. Once again, Merced County Social Services neglected to provide the post-adoption services they were paid to provide. Had these public officials done their jobs, Tom and his mother would have had some time to know each other before her death.

Cynthia Oka Perrett
(10/20/53 - 12/30/99)

*"You don't have to choose
between two families -
You just have a bigger family."*
-Search Story,
San Francisco Chronicle 11-19-98

9.
END OF THE SEARCH –
FOR FAMILY AND SELF

Because Tom's father, Tom Ralls, had an unlisted phone number, I went though the California Department of Motor Vehicles (DMV) messaging service, which, at the time, would, for a $5 fee, forward a message to the man whose name and year of birth matched the only Thomas Wayne Ralls on their computer system as holding a California driver's license. That service was later discontinued, but fortunately at that time, DMV did transmit the message and the resulting address was current.

Even more fortunate was finding a compassionate sounding man who was eager to meet his son - I heard back from Tom Sr. by phone, as soon as he received my message.

He lived in Suisun, only about 30 miles from Tom's prison - and he said he would try to visit Tom the next day and wanted to help Tom in any way he could.   I informed Tom's father that his mother had just died before he could see her. He didn't offer his street address or phone number (we didn't have cell phones then, so no way to see the phone number), and I didn't press him for it, since he had my phone number and Tom's location. He wanted to first be certain that Tom *was* his son.

In case getting a firsthand close look at each other wasn't enough, DNA testing was available and Tom already had a DNA paternity test in connection with his daughter.

On Saturday, the prison denied Tom's father a visit and he was handed a Visitor Application form that would take 3 weeks to process, despite that he explained the circumstances. If a dying mother had not been a compelling reason a week before, a father-son reunion wasn't going to cut any ice either.

91

But the determined father was willing to wait and to keep trying in the meantime.

Ralls kept in touch with me, volunteering more background about himself and Tom's mother.

He said Tom's mother did have problems, but they probably stemmed from the fact that she was sexually abused as a child. Even so, he is sure that she loved all of her children, including Tom, and didn't want to lose him.

Although Tom Jr's parents lived together for a long time, they were never married to each other. When they separated, Ralls had doubted whether Tom Jr. was actually his son, which explained his reluctance to disclose his contact information until he could be certain. In the meantime, Ralls obtained an email address to stay in touch with me and a mail-drop box so he and Tom Jr. could exchange correspondence. So I scanned Tom's mug shots that Tom sent me and e-mailed them to Ralls with a one-line message:

"Any resemblance?"

A day or two later, I received this reply: "My wife informed me that I received some photos yesterday and in reviewing them it seems we probably know who Tommy's father is. When you get the photo I'm sending you, let me know what you think and I will reveal who is in the photo." A few days later, I received a photo in the mail from Ralls - one of himself taken when he was Tom Jr's age. I replied by e-mail:

"I think you've found your son!"

I then sent the side-by-side photos to Tom Jr. His reaction was:

"I think you've found my father!"

On May 29, 2000, Ralls e-mailed me an update:

> "Hi, Lori. Thought you might like to know I got to visit with Tom yesterday and had a real nice visit. Thanks again for all you have done."

92

Tom McGee had been free of illicit drugs for more than a year when he paroled on April 23, 2001. He was not starting a "new" life. He was starting *life*.

Good luck Tom.

Tom McGee, 2001

PART 3:

MORE
ADDICTED
ADOPTEES

9 OUT OF 10

PEOPLE WITH SUBSTANCE PROBLEMS
STARTED USING BY AGE 18

Lifetime prevalence rates of illicit substance use disorder (SUDs) are about **43% higher among adoptees** than non-adoptees:
- 41% for alcohol, compared to 27.5% among non-adoptees;
- 25.4% for adoptees, 16.1% for non-adoptees for nicotine;
- 2.9% for opioids, 1.3% for non-adoptees;
- 3.2% for cannabis for adoptees, 7.6% for non-adoptees.

--Patrick M. Burns, *"The Adjustment of Adoptees,"* Psychology Today, 3-31-15

ADOPTEES, ABUSE, ADDICTION
and MENTAL ILLNESS

Researchers have linked physical, sexual and emotional child abuse with addiction.

"Almost all children who enter an out-of-home placement, away from their birth parents, struggle with being able to trust adults, usually have poor social skills, and often feel as if they are the only child who does not live with their birth parents." (--Source: Center for Adoption Support and Education-CASE).

According to recovering addicts and counselors involved in the famed "Delancey Street" model drug rehab program:

"Drug abuse is usually a side effect of a much deeper behavior flaw or reaction that must be pin-pointed and addressed before reaching a healthy, maintainable level of recovery."

Another successful drug and alcohol treatment program, "Passages Malibu," is based on the philosophy that drug and alcohol dependency is not a "disease." Treatment focuses on the 4 causes of addiction and these 4 conditions also describe circumstances under which many *adoptees* try to cope:

- chemical imbalance;
- events of the past you have not resolved;
- current conditions you can't cope with;
- things you believe that aren't true.

Addiction can also be the long term side effect of prescribed drugs such as Ritalin, routinely prescribed to "manage" fostered and adopted children's behaviors in the same way that the mentally ill, including those incarcerated, are "managed" with chemical restraints and who self-medicate, and as the following adoptees have experienced.

ACKERMAN, Gerald "Ajax"

Born to an alcoholic mother, Ackerman was taken from her by the State and adopted at 18 months. He grew up troubled in Oak Park, Michigan, described by his own adoptive sister, DeAnn Fierman, as "the evilest child" she had ever seen.

On June 20, 2000, Gerald "Ajax" Ackerman, 42, an adoptee who was the Mayor of Port Huron, Michigan, was sentenced on 16 felony counts stemming from sexual activities with girls 9 to 14. Ackerman, a former biker, is said to have brought more of the "common folk" into city government and helped reduce gang problems. He was also director of "Clear Choices," a center that counseled troubled youths to keep them off drugs. It was at the Center that Ackerman ran into trouble by having sex with the young girls there, police said. His attorney, Gerry Mason, said it was a tragedy for Ackerman, a man who it appeared had taken a lost life and turned it around. Gene Schabeth and Janet Naylor (The Detroit News, 4-8-99) profiled Ackerman who rose from drug addiction to public office. Ackerman began using drugs and alcohol at age 14 in high school when his adoptive parents sent him away to military school in Illinois. To an already troubled adoptee, being sent away from home equates to another "rejection," compounding the perceived "rejection" by his parents despite that he was not voluntarily relinquished. He managed to graduate Allendale High but failed at college and Navy enlistment. His frequent run-ins with the law began at age 15 continued until he was 30. It took a near-fatal car crash, the breakup of his first marriage, and 5 trips to rehab to get himself cleaned up.

"Ajax" is the name he picked up during his biker days, from the movie "The Warriors." His behavior so disturbed his adoptive parents that they gave up on him and moved to Florida—which he must have regarded as one more rejection. By the time Ackerman arrived in Port Huron in 1987, he was clean of drugs and alcohol and apparently was determined to remake his life, but he was homeless. He was able to borrow money to attend St. Clair College and graduated with an Associates in Arts (AA) degree.

In 1994, Ackerman was named "Michigan Public Citizen of the Year" by the National Association of Social Workers, becoming their "adoptee success story" poster boy.

98

At the time of his 1999 arrest and resignation from office, he was only 6 credits shy of a Bachelor's degree from Eastern Michigan University. Just as the 2000 presidential election will always be a subject of controversy, so was the verdict by Ackerman's jury. In 2002, this author wrote to Ackerman inquiring whether he had ever reconnected with his parents or had any desire to, and whether he would like to comment for publication. He did not reply. (Sources: Article by Gene Schabeth and Janet Naylor, The Detroit News, 4-8-99; and *"Former Mayor Gerald 'Ajax' Ackerman Will Spend at Least 18 Years in Prison for Sexual Misconduct Involving Children,"* AP,; Maryann George, Detroit Free Press)

BOWLES, Gary Ray *("he Florida Gay Bar Murders")*

Born 1-25-62, in Clifton Forge, Virginia, the second son of Frances Carole Price Bowles, Gary's was a stepparent adoption. His biological father, William Frank Bowles, died in 1961 before he was born. Frances remarried several times. At age 7 or 8, Gary began to suffer from abuse by his first stepfather and later by subsequent stepfathers. Around age 10, Gary began to sniff glue and paint, as well as experiment with drugs in an attempt to escape his unhappy situation, and dropped out of school during the 8th grade. When he was 13 or 14, Gary and his brother ganged up on their stepfather, severely beat him, then left home to live on the streets. Throughout his youth and adulthood he was able to provide for himself financially by prostituting himself to men and remained homeless for a majority of his teenage years and adulthood. He was not gay but was violent in his relationships with women. Gary Bowles is on Death Row at Union Correctional Institute - Raiford, Florida, awaiting execution on 3 counts of First Degree Murder (Source: *"Crime Library)"*

CATLIN, Steven, David 19

Born in 1944, Steven Catlin was adopted as an infant by Glenn and Martha Rose Catlin, of Fresno, California, and raised in Bakersfield. His first arrest was at age 19 for Forgery and Theft after he dropped out of school and was drug addicted. Over time, he murdered several people, including both of his adoptive parents – Martha in 1976, and Glenn in 1980, and 2 of his 6 wives, Joyce Adeline Catlin and Glenda Kay Catlin - with Paraquat poison

- undiscovered because he had their bodies quickly cremated. He was convicted of Murder and sentenced to Life in prison, with other charges pending. (--Source: crimezzz.net/serialkillers/)

CHIZUM, Max Alan

Max was born a "Christmas baby" on December 25, 1956 in South Bend, Indiana, to a single mom when the "unwed mother" in America was still considered a "disgrace" and her child was still an "illegitimate" or "bastard."

When Max's parents first met in South Bend, his father had been separated from his wife and their one child. He left South Bend before he knew that she was pregnant with Max. Because Max's birth was premature, he had to be on a respirator at first. He was then placed with foster parents named "Hoy" and his adoption was finalized in St. Joseph County, Indiana, in 1957.

During his childhood, Max was sexually abused by his adoptive father.

When Max attained legal age in Indiana, he was still prohibited by law from knowing who his natural parents were, but he was able to learn from the St. Joseph Probate Court's "non-identifying information" that his grandparents were both killed in an auto accident and that his mother completed night school after Max was born. She had training as a commercial artist, having done work for the US Navy, also had training as an X-ray apprentice draftsman, and went to live with an aunt in Peru, Indiana. Max's biological father was said to be a truck driver. As for his biological mother, his now-deceased adoptive father once told him that he saw a letter in a "Dear Abby" or "Ann Landers" newspaper advice column from a woman *"seeking information about a child born on Christmas 1956 in South Bend–Want you back–Mistake."* But there was no effort to track down the source.

Max was convicted for dealing 3.5 grams of Methamphetamine and was sentenced to 40 years with earliest release date in 2019. He detoxed "cold turkey" while in prison. Max had been married, has five children and two grandchildren.

He wrote to AmFOR: "The emotional side of this, of being alone and disconnected, and not fitting in, is only one side of the coin. The other side is that my children and their children should have access to their and their family's medical history and true background information." (--Source: Max Chizum's letters to AmFOR)

CLAIR, Tiffany

Tiffany Clair was conceived of rape, adopted at birth, attempted suicide and shot up drugs together with her adoptive mother when she overdosed and died at age 15. Her adoptive mother, Debra Gatlin Clair, went on trial for Manslaughter in the March 3, 2001 death of her adopted daughter.

CORNE, James

A severely depressed and schizophrenic drug user, Corne used a butcher knife to his 54 year old adoptive mother, Peggy Corne, as horrified family members watched, stabbed her to death. Corne told Auburn, Washington police she "pushed his buttons" and made him angry. (Source: Nancy Bartley, "*Man Gets 22 Years for Killing Mother*," Seattle Times, 3-24-01)

COTTON, Marcus B., 22

Born February 28, 1974, Marcus Cotton was on drugs since age 5 as result of his adoptive father being drug addicted and habitually abusing him and his siblings. He completed 9th grade, worked as a laborer, had convictions for Drug Possession and Attempted Murder prior to his conviction in 1996 for the shooting death of Assistant District Attorney Gil Epstein, 27, during a robbery when he found Epstein's badge while robbing him in a parking lot. Cotton was executed in Texas. (--Source: Houston Chronicle, 11-5-97; Texas Department of Criminal Justice Offender Information website)

DiLORENZO, Melody

At age 24, Melody was hospitalized in critical condition from multiple stab wounds allegedly inflicted by an assailant as result of a drug deal gone bad. ("*Desert Hot Springs Woman Stabbed*," by Stephanie McKinnon, Staff Writer, The Desert Sun, 8-7-93). But Sheila Grove, Melody's adoptive mother, said that Melody's wounds were self-inflicted – one of several suicide attempts of the past three years ("*Why I'm Anti-Adoption*" by Sheila Grove, LoriCarangelo.com/Adopters). From her hospital bed, Melody told me she wanted to find her natural mother. I pulled some strings and mother and daughter were reunited within 24 hours and began a long healing process. (--Source: Melody DiLorenzo and Sheila Grove)

DU PLOOY, Schalk, 18

Schalk Du Plooy, *drug addicted* and alcoholic since age 12, murdered his adoptive parents, Schalk Du Plooy, Sr., 62, and Theresa Du Plooy, 51, both alcoholic, *drug addicted pharmacists*, in Johannesburg, South Africa. Just before the murders, his adoptive parents told him *they regretted adopting him and that he "should leave."* (--Source: Jeanne-Marie Versluis, "*Addict Guilty of Killing Adoptive Parents,* " News24, 11-3-11)

DYER, Michael Daniel

Michael was born August 30, 1966 in Monticello, Indiana, under the name Michael Daniel Woggerman. He was adopted by Donald Wayne and Joyce Marie Dyer in 1971 through the Tehama County Superior Court in Red Bluff, California.

Michael shared that his adoptive parents, who he referred to as "old school Christians," no longer want a relationship with him due to his past behaviors and incarceration, and have always claimed they "know nothing" about his natural family. The Social Services record showed that although he had been taken from his parents for neglect, had to go on welfare, and his two sisters were also adopted out. Michael was raised in Oregon and had many unanswered questions about his pre-adoption past. Although a 1971 physician's record indicates Michael had been severely beaten in infancy, it is unknown whether, if true, the abuse occurred while he was in foster care, or whether he had an abusive parent, because the same record also indicates "no negligence" and that he received appropriate medical care and immunizations.

In 1971, when his adoptive parents returned to court, his father also appeared in court and indicated that he wanted to have Michael and Michael's siblings returned to him. But the court or agency opined that, despite that his father "made a gesture of financial support for him," his father "showed little if any affection" toward him and his siblings, calling the father's attitude "sterile" as an excuse for refusing to stop the adoptions. Michael described himself as always having been obsessively disciplined in his personal hygiene, dress and housekeeping, and wondered if that might be inherited. He said that, in adulthood, he felt trapped in a self-made prison from an insatiable need for sex (but committed no sex crimes and believes in treating women with the utmost respect), money (he did steal and was convicted of Petty Theft with Priors), and drugs. Because, in childhood, he was diagnosed as having Attention Deficit Disorder, it is likely that he was treated with prescription drugs such as Ritalin, which has led many adoptees use of street drugs. In 2010 Michael contacted AmFOR in hope of finding his natural family. Because Michael knows his birth name is "Woggerman," he sent a simple letter to all Woggermans listed in Oregon but none responded, perhaps because of his prison address. (--Source: Michael Dyer's letters to AmFOR).

ERSKINE, Robert *(aka Chevalier)*

"Rob" was born June 5, 1967 under his birth name, Robert Lee Fields, at Queen of the Valley Hospital in Napa, California, to Beth Sabin and Floyd Fields. Rob is of German, Scottish, Irish and Native American descent. At age 1-1/2, his parents relinquished him for adoption, but it was not until he was 6 that he was adopted in Santa Rosa (Sonoma County), California, by Dale and Sharon Erskine.

Rob shared that he was unhappy with his adoptive family. He dropped out of high school in 10th grade and suffered severe head trauma from an auto accident in 2008. Rob first wrote to AmFOR from a Montana prison in 2001 in hope of finding his mother and was not heard from again until 2009 when he was incarcerated at Oregon State Hospital in Salem, Oregon, where he has access to prescription drug treatment. (--Source: Robert Erskine's letters to AmFOR)

HEATER, Naomi Kimberly

Naomi Heater, 27, was adopted as an infant from South Korea. She had a long standing drug problem and was enraged over her adoptive parents' decision to take away her pickup truck. Naomi had saved her adoptive mother's life by donating a kidney for a transplant operation. Six years later, she killed her adoptive mother.

HELM, Roger Scott

Born June 13, 1969 in Arizona, Roger was 14 when he was tried "as an adult" for the murders of both of his adoptive parents and his 16-year old adoptive sister in their sleep while he was high on LSD. Roger says his adoptive parents viewed his adoptive sister as "could do no wrong" yet she had her own Adopted Child Syndrome problems, and viewed him as "could do no right."

Roger wrote to AmFOR:

> "My adoptive parents barred my windows, bugged the phones, probably afraid I might try to find my *real parents* and lied about who my 'real parents' were. I frequently ran away. That my adoption was at the root of my problems never occurred to me. The Public Defender had no interest in protecting a child's rights and interests in adult court. Instead, the focus was to convince the child to plead Guilty, which I eventually did and I was sentenced to 88 years."

Roger grew up in Arizona's toughest prisons where violence was a common presence, the environment one of confusion, hate, rape, despair and lack of compassion. Yet he has struggled to remain optimistic and positive. He obtained his GED and took college classes when they were available. He studied as much as he could to attempt his own appeals in Arizona's Superior Court, Appeals Court, and State Superior Court, but his inexperience was against him and the courts denied him a new trial.

AmFOR assisted Roger's lifelong search for his biological mother, Arlene Sharon Bell. But when she was told by prison officials why he was in prison, she refused contact with him, thus cutting off any possibility of locating his biological father or other family members. In Roger's 2004 letter, he said. "No one seems to comprehend the need to know who you are and where you came from. That's something only my Mom can answer. She's in no danger from me and if she doesn't want to know me, it's something I can accept because at least it was definitely said, ya know?" In 2009, he married while in prison, but she divorced him 9 months later.

Roger's case was riddled with errors that raise constitutional issues. His Public Defender did not bring out evidence or even investigate regarding the physical and mental abuse Roger endured from his adoptive family, nor considered the Adopted Child Syndrome defense that was successful in other cases of young adoptees who murdered their adoptive parents, and who were tried as juveniles and released at legal age. The Prosecutor sought the Death Penalty only after Roger refused 2 plea offers. The Public Defender's office passed him around from one attorney to another 3 times and those attorneys never fully researched his case. His attorney never presented evidence that a police officer lied about his confession, never made an audio or video tape of his interview, destroyed his original notes, and never informed the court that Roger was questioned without an attorney present, was under the influence of LSD and was coerced by police. (Source: Helm's letters to AmFOR)

HITTLE, Daniel Joe

Born March 1, 1950 in Indiana, Daniel Hittle completed 14 years of school and worked as a welder. In 1973, in Minnesota, he killed his adoptive parents. He served 11 years in prison and was paroled in 1984. In 1989 after a feud with his drug dealer and his wife, he began shooting at police, killing an officer before surrendering. Hittle was executed 12-6-00 at Huntsville, Texas. (Source: David Carson, December Press, 12-13-00; clarkprosecutor.org; Texas Dept. of Criminal Justice Offender website)

HOWARD, Aaron

Aaron Howard, an African-American adoptee, was found guilty of Second Degree Murder in the brutal 6-12-07 slaying of his Caucasian female adoptive parents, Deborah Frankel-Howard, 61, in their west-end home in Ottawa, Canada. He was originally charged with First Degree Murder but The Crown was not able to prove the murder was premeditated. The young man sat expressionless in the courtroom and did not react much when the guilty plea was entered. Deborah Frankel-Howard had worked many years for Health Canada. She was found dead inside her home after family and neighbors noticed they had not seen her in several days. Howard had often argued with his adoptive parents. Apparently in a rage one day, he bludgeoned her with a lead pipe. He then carried her body to a cold storage room in the basement and left her there for a week with the air-conditioning running. At the time of the murder, Aaron Howard began what he described as "an orgy of sex, drugs and rock 'n' roll," according to an excerpt from his diary that was part of a statement of facts submitted to the court. Howard revealed in his diary "In a fit of *anger* and insanity I brutally murdered my mother." (Source: Tony Lofaro, Ottawa News, DOSE.ca)

HUDSON, Deanna

Deanna Hudson, an adoptee, was 30-years old when she provided her story to AmFOR as follows:

"I was Deanne Lorraine Harper at birth, the oldest of three girls. My father was shot and killed by the man who my mother married when I was 3-1/2. He adopted me and my sister and later another daughter who was his and my mother's biological child. I remember us moving to California when I was six. Things seemed pretty good until my Mom caught my adoptive father cheating on her. She beat him up and threw him out. From then on, a lot of men were coming and going. Unknown to my mother, her boyfriends started molesting me.

One night I was raped and told my mother what happened. She beat me bad, and when I went to school the next day with bruises and choke marks on my neck the teacher called Social Services and I was placed in foster care. The foster parents were very mean to me, so I believed it was all my fault that I got raped and later the court sent me back home where I was continually molested by men my mother knew. I was back and forth between foster homes and my mother, until I became pregnant.

When I was sent to prison for selling drugs, a lady from Social Services told me I had to sign over my son for adoption while in prison or she would have me charged with being unfit and make sure I lost him permanently. I didn't want him to end up going from one foster home to another so I signed, not realizing I would not be permitted to see him again or know where he is. He was born January 10, 1986 in Visalia, California. Even though my son was with a babysitter when I was doing drugs, I know I was doing wrong but want him to know the reasons, and that I never stopped loving him."

JOBS, Steve

Historically, pro-adoption writers have made any "successful" adoptee a "poster child" for adoption. When adoptee Steve Jobs, co-founder and CEO of Apple Computer, died at age 56 on 10-5-11, Greg Gutfeld put such a spin on his October 6, 2011 article for FOXNewsInsider.com titled *"What if Steve Jobs' Birth Mother Had Chosen an Option Other Than Adoption?"*

Gutfeld wrote that her father [Jobs' grandfather] "didn't want his daughter marrying a Syrian, so her baby was put up for adoption by a working class couple who encouraged his interest in technology." And that Steve's mother was a "hero" for giving him up for adoption "instead of choosing a more finite option." Gutfeld pondered, "Imagine what a hole there would be in this world if she went the other way." Following is what Gutfeld left out of his snapshot of this adoptee's alleged idyllic adopted life - and why Jobs is more appropriately a poster child for Adopted Child Syndrome:

Steven Paul Jobs was born February 25, 1955 to Joanne Simpson and Abdulfattah "John" Jandali, two unmarried University of Wisconsin graduate students who gave him up for adoption. His mother worked as a speech therapist and his Syrian father was a political science professor. Shortly after being placed for adoption, his biological parents married and had another child, Mona Simpson, who became a well known novelist. Earlier in his life, Jobs was quoted as saying that he had felt *"an unresolved pain over being adopted,"* and *"always had a feeling of abandonment,"* yet, in denial of those feelings, he said on tape to his authorized biographer, Walter Isaacson, that being told by his adoptive parents that he was "special" because he had been "chosen" made him "feel positive about himself"... so "positive" that he dropped out of college and out of life, as an under-achieving hippie, traveled to India to seek enlightenment, and to The Primal Therapy Center in Eugene, Oregon, for a radical form of psychotherapy... and used various mind-altering drugs, including LSD.

Still obsessed with finding his origins, Jobs finally hired a private investigator to locate his mother. To varying degrees, most adoptees endure perilous journeys en-route to their pasts. It was not until Jobs was 27 that he was able to uncover information about his biological parents, and met his mother and sister.

But although he once shook his biological father's hand at the restaurant his father owned and where the man bragged that Steve Jobs had eaten there, he never revealed to the man that he was his son and forbid his sister from doing so, saying it was because he had "heard something he didn't like about him." Was Jobs, described as "normally confrontational," so resentful of his father for letting his mother give him up for adoption that he could not confront him? Or did he derive satisfaction from keeping himself secret from the man, as his father and his adoptive parents had been kept secret from him?

Before that, at age 23, Steve Jobs fathered a daughter, Lisa, with his girlfriend, Chrisann Brennan, but denied paternity alleging he was sterile to avoid child support, until the court intervened. Is it any coincidence that until he found his biological parents and had his lifelong questions answered that he *then* initiated a relationship with his daughter when she was 7... and that it was not until 1991 that he married Laurene Powell, a Stanford MBA student and eventually had 3 children with her? It would appear that, while Steve Jobs exhibited his creative intelligence, inherited from his biological parents, and, along with his work addiction, it helped him succeed as an entrepreneur in a highly competitive technical field, it was not until he solved the mystery of his pre-adoption existence that he matured *socially* although described by his employees as "cold," and as a "control freak" who parked in handicap spaces and refused to have a license plate on his car.

In Steve Jobs' commencement address at Stanford University, in the part that media *did not air*, Jobs, who never graduated from college, spoke of his biological mother and how his adoptive parents, who had been on a waiting list for a child to adopt, received a phone call in the middle of the night asking: 'We have an unexpected baby boy. Do you want him?'" So much for the "chosen child" story.
Jobs went on:

> "My biological mother later found out that my [adoptive] mother never graduated from college and that my [adoptive] father never graduated from high school. She refused to sign

the final adoption papers. She only relented a few months later when my [adoptive] parents promised I would someday go to college."

Although he resumed college 17 years later, he said he dropped out again, because it was costing his working class [adoptive] parents all of their savings. and he had "no goal" in mind. Many adoptees intentionally resist being morphed into the child that their adoptive parents could not have of their own. And, knowing his cancer had spread, Jobs advised the graduating students:

"Your time is limited *so don't waste it living someone else's life.* Don't be trapped by dogma – which is living with the results of other people's thinking. Have the courage to follow your heart and intuition. They somehow already know what you truly want to become."

Steve Jobs grew up struggling with "not knowing" and being unable to gain insight into who he was, unresolved by drugs, psychotherapy, work, nor multi-billionaire wealth. Had almost 3 decades of his life not been burdened and preoccupied with uncovering the secrecy of his origins, confidence to set goals and have a relationship with his daughter may have found expression decades sooner. (--Source: *"The Journey is the Reward,"* by Jeffrey S. Young; and Stanford University News *"You've Got to Find What You Love,"* transcript, Stanford Report, 6-14-06; *and "Steve Jobs Biography"* Synopsis, Biography.com; and CBS-60 Minutes transcript, 10-23-11.)

JONES, Timothy Jason, 29

Born 6-23-75, in Alabama, Timothy Jones murdered his adoptive parents, Dr. Timothy Jones, Sr., 31, and Nancy Jones, in January 2004. He was arrested after co-workers reported that Tim Sr, 31, was late to work. Tim Sr. had been beaten and repeatedly stabbed in the carport of the house and his wife, Nancy, lay battered beyond recognition in her bed. Jason Jones was caught later that day driving his adoptive parents' car in north Alabama. He crashed the car after fleeing from police. Neighbors said the young man had spent years in and out of various rehabilitation clinics for drug addiction.

The night before their murders, his adoptive parents had taken away a family-owned sports utility vehicle from Timothy. According to trial testimony, when police who were called to the home previously that day, Timothy was belligerent and brandishing a knife in the Jones' yard. Police took him across town and dropped off at a telephone booth as his adoptive parents requested. Later in the night, he returned to the Jones' home, but elder Jones locked him in a basement room at his adoptive grandparents' vacant home. He later broke out of the home, walked back to his adoptive parents' house, and attacked Tim Sr. as he was leaving for work in the early morning. He then attacked his adoptive mother with a weapon he told police he fashioned from pipe and other objects at his adoptive grandparents' house.

Nancy Jones was beaten so savagely that parts of her jaw and teeth were found scattered across the room. Tim told police in taped statements that he took money from her purse and bought crack cocaine, smoking it in the house before fleeing. He was convicted of Capital Murder by a Jefferson County jury and sentenced to Death, In his last statement to the jury, Jones said "I'm a monster. I have no remorse for what I did. I deserve to die."

He had registered on PrisonerLife.com seeking penpals. His attorney, John Wiley, had never provided him with his requested trial transcripts, never informed him of court decisions, never returned his calls. Another website states the Prosecutor at his trial told the jury he was a 'monster.' Soon afterward, he committed suicide at Holman maximum security prison. (Source: Connie Baggett, Mobile Register Alabama 9-3-06).

LOPEZ, Ronald Leo

Ron wrote AmFOR:

> "I was 13 months old and my brother was 2 when my Dad went to prison. When he was released from prison and remarried, my father evidently fought for custody of us when Social Services took us from our mother, and for a time we were adopted by this new stepmother. Over time, I had lots of hate towards my real parents though I was too young to remember who they were. I just knew I hated them for abandoning me and my brother and for letting my

brother and me become separated. I was sent to several foster homes and when I was older it was group homes. I found it hard to trust anyone. At 17, I was legally on my own and lived on the streets where I quickly grew up and quickly got into drugs. Drugs took away my emotional roller-coaster. Of course I stole to pay for drugs, and was in and out of hospitals, drug programs, and prisons, and am now in this prison on a 'Three Strikes' sentence of 25-years-to-Life."

MANNEX, Russell

Russ was born 9-25-65 as Shannon P. Smith at Saint Anne's Convent in Santa Ana, California. Since 1999, Russ has been serving his 10-year sentence for Attempted Rape and had a history of alcohol and drug abuse. He was incarcerated in 2001 at California's "model" Substance Abuse Treatment Facility at Corcoran State Prison in California in 2001 when he wrote AmFOR:

"During my childhood, my adoptive parents were always honest with us about our adoptions, making sure to explain that we had been "chosen" which made us "special." However, I never felt "special. " I felt "different "and often ruminated on thoughts of being "rejected." I became very hurt inside despite the love offered by my adoptive parents. I experienced further alienation when I began noticing I had feelings for other guys. I suppressed my sexual orientation because growing up in a conservative community made it impossible for me to express my concerns, so these feelings were never discussed.

I was adopted at the age of 2 months and know absolutely nothing about my biological parents except for their nationality. According to the adoption agency, my mother was too young to raise me and her conservative family believed the best option was to send her to a convent and allow her baby to be adopted. My dad is East Indian and my mom is 1/4 Italian and 1/4 Irish. When I was on the outside, I always worked and tried to spend a lot of time with my wife and son but made a mistake and now have a 12-year sentence. For whatever it's worth, I am in no way angry at my parents for giving me up for adoption. I love them even though I have never known them.

Thank you for working with adoptees, including those of us who are incarcerated. I've tried to make sense as to why I did not feel loved by my adoptive parents. I ran away from home at age 5 because of physical and emotional abuse as result of their alcoholism and not considering me one of their own. I felt unloved, unworthy, guilt, shame, anger, resentment, fear of abandonment, rejection, denial and distrust, all at the same time.

By age 8, I began serious lying and set a field on fire which was only a hundred yards from our house. I wanted to "belong," and tried to cloud my feelings. If I would just hint that I wanted to know about my biological parents, I'd get a negative reaction.

I began to use and sell marijuana, and, at age 16, I attempted suicide by swallowing 40 Valium pills with turpentine. But before I could completely load my shotgun to finish the job, I passed out and awoke in a Detention Center a week or so later, where I self-inflicted stab wounds and refused to eat. I was ordered by the court to see a psychologist for six months. But within a couple months, the psychologist—the first person I had begun to trust—molested me. Shortly afterward, a teacher and a friend of the family both molested me. I continued lying, stealing, smoking and selling pot, truancy, withdrawal from people, promiscuity and self destructive behaviors in general. I managed to enter the military at age 17 and, from then on, nurtured a work addiction as a way to gain acceptance and a sense of self-worth. Despite an honorable discharge, my criminal thinking continued. My first wife and I ended up in a federal prison for counterfeiting U.S. currency. Five years after my release, I began this sentence of 7 to 15 years in 1994 for Attempted Rape. Since late 1997, I have been a cancer survivor in search of my past—still trying to fill an empty hole. God help me.

Then one day my biological mother and my brother (her other son) found me through AmFOR's Adopted Prisoners website. Finally, I heard a Texas accent on the phone and we've been in communication ever since. At first, she had some difficulty with my being Gay. But we are hoping I can go to Texas to visit her when I'm out, or possibly even transfer my parole. Connecting with my mother has changed my life. The only 'loose end' is finding my father, Thomas Phillips Smith. I hope to some day finally meet him. Thank you for your help over the years. You have given me a beautiful gift."

In 2010, I was surprised to receive an e-mail from Russ informing me he had been released from prison, was looking for work, and hoped to visit his mother in Texas when he could afford to. I didn't hear further until 2011 when his adoptive mother, Lorraine Mannex, phoned me to thank me for helping Russ find his natural mother. She said it has had a positive impact on his life and that all was going well for Russ.

O'CONNOR, Hugh

Hugh was born in Rome, Italy, and adopted when he was 6 days old by actor Carrol O'Connor ("*In the Heat of the Night*," and "*All In the Family*") and his wife, Nancy. Hugh was named after Carroll O'Connor's brother who died in a motorcycle accident in 1961. When he was 16, Hugh was diagnosed with Hodgkins Lymphoma. He survived the cancer and two surgeries, but had been taking prescription drugs for the pain and marijuana for nausea and became addicted to harder drugs. Despite numerous stays at rehab clinics, he never conquered his addiction. On March 28, 1995, Hugh called his father to tell him he was going to end his life; he said he believed he could not beat drugs nor face another drug rehab program. Carroll called police who arrived at Hugh's Pacific Palisades home just as he shot himself in the head. Police later determined he had cocaine in his blood. (Source: Wikipedia)

OKEN, Steven Howard

Born January 22, 1962, Steve Oken was adopted at birth by David and Davida Oken. Steve had become drug addicted, stealing drugs from the pharmacy owned and operated by his adoptive parents. Two weeks after murdering his adoptive mother, Oken sexually assaulted and killed his wife's older sister, Patricia Antoinette Hirt, then fled to Maine where he sexually assaulted and killed Lori Elizabeth Ward, a college student. He claimed to have amnesia when apprehended but regained his memory when convicted of Garvin's murder. After his sentencing, defense therapists testified that he suffered from "a rare case of sexual sadism."

Steven Oken was executed in Maryland on June 17, 2004 at age 42, as result of 1991 convictions for the 1987 murders of the 3 women. Steve's adoptive parents told media they were committed to stand by their adopted son but did not attend his execution. (--Source: Alice Kim, *"Help Save My Son!"* Baltimore Sun, 2-6-03; *"Campaign to End the Death Penalty,"* The New Abolitionist)

PURDY, Patrick Edward *(Stockton Elementary School Massacre)*

Patrick Edward Purdy was born on November 10, 1964 in Tacoma, Washington. His father, Patrick Benjamin Purdy, was a staff sergeant in the Army and was stationed at Fort Lewis at that time of his son's birth. His mother was Kathleen Toscano. When Patrick was 2 years old, his mother divorced her husband after he had threatened her with a weapon, and Kathleen moved with her son to South Lake Tahoe, and later to the Sacramento area.

The Cleveland Elementary School Massacre in Stockton, California, was an incident of mass murder that occurred on January 17, 1989. The gunman, Patrick Purdy, then a disturbed drifter and former Stockton resident who held a long criminal history, shot and killed five school children, and wounded 29 other school children and one teacher, before committing suicide. He had attended Cleveland Elementary School from kindergarten through second grade. Patrick's mother remarried though was again divorced five years later. Albert Gulart, Purdy's stepfather, said Patrick was an overly quiet child who couldn't cope with things and according to his aunt, he was an alcoholic during his childhood. When Purdy was thirteen, he once struck his mother in the face and therefore was permanently thrown out of her house. Purdy began living on the streets of San Francisco for a while, before being placed in foster care.

Purdy was adopted shortly after (between age 13 and 14), and settled with his foster family in the West Hollywood area. There, he became a drug addict and went to high school only sporadically. Purdy had a long criminal history, which began during early adolescence. In order to support his drug addiction, he became a prostitute, which resulted in his first arrest in 1980. He was later arrested in 1982 for possession of marijuana and drug dealing, in 1983 for possession of an illegal weapon and receipt of stolen property.

In October 1984 he was arrested for being an accomplice in an armed robbery, and spent 32 days in the Yolo County Jail. In 1986 his adoptive mother called police when he vandalized her car, after she refused to give him money for drugs.

In April 1987, he was once more arrested for firing a semi-automatic pistol at trees in the Eldorado National Forest. At the time, he was carrying a book about the white supremacist group Aryan Nations.

Later in jail he tried to commit suicide twice, once by hanging himself with a rope made out of strips of his shirt, and a second time by cutting his wrists with his fingernails.

A subsequent psychiatric assessment found him to suffer from mild mental retardation, and to be a danger to himself and others.

In October 1987 he left and drifted between Oregon, Nevada, Texas, Florida, Connecticut, South Carolina, and Tennessee searching for work. He eventually returned to California where he rented a room at the El Rancho Motel in Stockton on December 26th. After the school shooting, the room was found decorated with numerous toy soldiers. His hatred was especially directed against Vietnamese and other Asian immigrants, stating that they take away jobs from native-born Americans, while he himself struggled to

get along. According to his friends, who described him as nice and never violent towards anyone, Purdy was suicidal at times and upset and mad about the fact that he failed to "make it on his own." In a notebook, found in a hotel where he lived in early 1988, Purdy wrote about himself in a self-loathing perspective: *"I'm so dumb, I'm dumber than a sixth-grader. My mother and father were dumb."* (Source: Murderpedia)

QUINLAN, Karen Ann

Karen Ann Quinlan, an adoptee, made national headlines when she fell into a coma for 10 years from over-dosing on drugs and alcohol. Her journal reflects possible thoughts of suicide:

> "I wish to curl myself into a fetal pose
> and rest in the eternal womb awhile."

Society became distracted by the legalisms surrounding whether Quinlan's life support machine should be disconnected and whether she had "the right to *die with dignity*." The question as to whether adoptees like Quinlan have the right to *life with dignity* from knowing their own origins was never mentioned. (--Source: "*Karen Ann* " *Tells Her Story*," Doubleday, 1977).

SHELLMAN, James

Jimmy Shellman was 11 years old when he killed a 9-year old girl near Afton, Oklahoma, in 1958, and hid the body. He said it happened while in a rage from upon learning his adoptive parents was actually his biological aunt. He confessed to the crime 45 years later, in 2003, when he was 56, after a conviction on Burglary and drug charges, at the Veterans Affairs hospital in Joplin, Missouri. (Source: "*Delaware County Man Confesses to 1958 Slaying*," NewsOK.com, 10-7-03.)

SPENCER, Brenda *(The Cleveland Elementary School Shooter)*

Born 4-3-62, Brenda Spencer lived with her divorced father, who bought her the gun for Christmas that she used in her 1-29-79 spree killing at Cleveland Elementary school, killing 2 and injuring 9 students. It was said to have been her reaction to her parents' separation and she had been involved with drugs and petty theft and was addicted to violent films. -- (Source: Brian Lane and Wilfred Gregg, "*Encyclopedia of Mass Murder*," Brockhampton Press, 1994)

SMITH, Kevin Douglas

Born 7-17-63 in Kern County, California, Kevin was serving a 31-year sentence with possibility of parole– 6 for Robbery, 5 for the gun enhancement, 20 for four 5-year prior enhancements for "robbing drug dealers" when he was a kid – when he first contacted AmFOR in 1996 at age 38. A burley biker who referred to himself as "Ole Honey Bear," Kevin has lived a fantasy life of "devil may care" excesses that have been categorized as Adopted Child Syndrome behaviors.

116

They include his past sexual exploits, when he was young and living out a "Robin Hood" fantasy, and a shootout with a SWAT team during a robbery which could have taken his life. Kevin's aggressive survival instincts saved his life while in prison. Kevin explains, "I always thought life was about two things: possessions and sex; everything else was just a path to that. I was told I was 'special' and 'chosen' which are terms the kids on the playground don't use, if you know what I mean, but I did fight a lot as a kid over name calling about my adoptive status. I've never really been into chemicals other than "grass," but I have been pulling capers for money since I was a teenager and did distance myself a lot from normal ways of thinking. When I was older, whenever I would drop a hint to my adoptive parents that I was interested in knowing about my natural parents, they'd have a "scared horses" look that told me to drop the subject. And I was never told by Social Services or anyone that, as an adult adoptee, I have a right to certain "non-identifying information."

On 10-22-96, Kevin received his "non-identifying" background information and he was surprised to learn he has an older brother. In May, 1997, with AmFOR's help, Kevin and his mother were finally in contact. His mother was paraplegic from a car accident, so could not travel to the prison to share a face to face meeting, but they maintained a steady correspondence.

On 7-21-97, Kevin wrote: *"Received a quatrillion page letter from my Mom! She is so very much like me that it is scary! This is so neat! Did you see how similar our handwriting is? I thanked her for the greatest gift of all – life!"* Kevin grew up realizing that the trade-off for being a "chosen child " meant "don't ask, don't tell," at least not in his adoptive parents' presence. Like manyadoptees, Kevin searched in secret for answers regarding vital questions of his identity and his place in the world. In self defense rather than denial, he admitted to Adopted Child Syndrome behaviors – lying, conflict with authority, stealing, sexual acting out, fire-setting, etc. He discovered he had not inherited his criminality.

STROHMEYER, Jeremy

Adopted in 1980 at 18 months old, Jeremy was an 18-year old honor student when, on 5-25-97 he raped and killed 7-year old Sherrice Iverson--a stranger to Jeremy--in a Las Vegas casino restroom. While Jeremy was molesting the girl, he strangled her to stifle her screams, and because she was still breathing, he twisted her head in an attempt to break her neck. He later told police "I just wanted to experience death." He was convicted of Rape and Murder and sentenced to Life. His famed attorney, Leslie Abramson, defended him based on his "diminished capacity" due to prescribed drugs and he was allegedly on methamphetamine ("speed").

Jeremy said that he had sometimes played a game called "whore dragging" in which he fantasized that prostitutes were lured to his car, grabbed by their arms as the driver sped off, and dragged along the street until Jeremy let go. The media focused on the fact that more than 800 files of child pornography were found on Jeremy's computer. At the urging of his adoptive parents, Jeremy pled Guilty, a plea bargain that allowed him to avoid the Death Penalty.

A year after his conviction, a Los Angeles Times feature (7-19-98) revealed that Jeremy had kept his adoptive status hidden even from his close friends and that, as early as age 4, Jeremy would talk about wanting to find and help his mother, that his mother had a drug problem and was diagnosed as schizophrenic or alcohol dependent, and that his father had been incarcerated in California for most of the previous 10 years for drug-related problems. Abramson, to her credit, told media that Jeremy was "not a bad seed" – that he was "mentally gone" at the time of the crime –but no one will ever know whether a jury would have been swayed by either the "diminished capacity" defense or an Adopted Child Syndrome defense. His highly publicized case also highlighted adoption-caused patterns of behavior.

Jeremy's public statement was as follows:
"In trying to answer questions, I have had much help from my lawyers, my adoptive parents, and psychiatric experts. For some of us who were adopted, not knowing from whom or from where we came can wreck our lives. It can make us walking time bombs, full of rage we don't consciously experience. I was filled with anger and rage I couldn't understand. My recently found half-brother who knows our mother, and grew up seeing her, has avoided the pitfalls of drug and alcohol use. But our brother [also adopted] has been having some of the same problems I was having. Adopted kids like me, I now know, seek out rejection and believe on some level that no one will keep them. Had any of the 3 mental health

118

professionals I sought help and advice from even raised the issue of adoption, they might have treated me for the complications it caused in my life. What needs to be understood is that being adopted is not the same as being born into a family. Many adopted kids do feel the confusion and doubts about who they are–as I did. What's bad is not knowing what your genetic history is, or why you were given up for adoption in the first place. It shouldn't be as difficult as it is to find out about your roots. Had my adoptive parents not been led to believe the false popular myth that adoption is a non-issue, they might have suspected the existence of a secret shameful self inside me. They might have seen how serious my struggle with it was. Closed adoptions are dangerous. Isolation and lack of real relationships and communication with your family is a real destroyer."

On 10-24-99, John and Winnie Strohmeyer filed suit against Los Angeles County alleging that social workers deliberately withheld crucial information about his mother's mental illness that would have stopped them from adopting – despite that although they already had a biological daughter, Heather, when they decided they wanted to adopt a "hard-to-place" child, one who might otherwise be "unwanted"–a term which may have lingered in Jeremy's subconscious. (Source: AP)

STRUEBING, Kurt Alan

In April 1986 Kurt Struebing, a guitarist for his black metal band, and on drugs, killed his adoptive parents, Dalee Struebing, 53, with a hatchet and pair of scissors. He was sentenced to 12 years for Second Degree Murder and released in 1994. He re-formed his band, "NME," gained international fame, became a trusting friend and doting father of one son.

Kurt was killed at age 39 on 3-11-05 when he drove his car through 2 barriers and plunged 50 feet off the opening of a span bridge. Police investigators and motorists who saw the crash were puzzled why Struebing drove off the bridge. Friends said he didn't like to talk about his past and, for most it, "it didn't matter." Kurt's mission in life was to help others. "His humility was endearing" and "everybody respected the hell out of him." (Source: Seattle Times; seattlepi.com/)

SWARTZ, Michael

Michael was one of 3 children adopted by Kay and Robert Swartz because Kay could not have children of her own. Michael's older adoptive brother, Larry, was convicted of murdering their adoptive parents in 1984 when Kay had case workers remove Michael from their home. Michael had drug and behavioral problems that landed him in the Crownsville Center Hospital Center. In 1990, Michael was convicted First Degree Murder for helping to murder a Crownsville man over a jar of coins. He is serving time at the Maryland Correctional Institution at Hagerstown. (Source: *"The Second Life of Larry Swartz"* by MarylandMissing, WebSleuths; and *"A Sudden Fury"* by Leslie Walker)

WEISE, Jeff, 16 *(The Red Lake Shooter)*

Jeff Weise's father committed suicide. His mother was in a nursing home after an auto accident and his grandfather had been raising him. On March 23, 2005, while on a mega-dose of Prozac "for depression," Weise went on a rampage, shooting to death his grandfather and the grandfather's companion. Then, armed with 2 pistols and a shotgun, he killed 9 people and wounded 7 before shooting himself to death at his school on the Red Lake Indian Reservation, the nation's bloodiest school shooting since Columbine 6 years prior. (Source: antidepressantsfacts.com/)

ADDENDUM

"EVERYTHING YOU THOUGHT YOU KNEW ABOUT ABOUT ADDICTION IS WRONG"

--JOHANN HARI, journalist, The Independent and Huffington Post, and author of *"Chasing the Scream: The First and Last Days of the War on Drugs,"* traveled 30,000 miles to 18 countries to investigate drug addiction by Tracy Giez-Ramsay, The Observor, 11-27-17:

"If you had asked me when I started doing the research, 'What causes heroin addiction?', I would have looked at you like you were an idiot," the author confesses to the audience. "I would have said, 'Well, the clue's in the name, dummy. It's called *heroin* addiction, it's obviously caused by heroin'." We've been told this story so often, Hari says, that it has become part of our common sense.

The author's talk was a paean to Vancouver's Downtown Eastside which he encouraged the audience to be tremendously proud of. Hari relayed the deep impact the community had on him both professionally and personally. "I'm genuinely glad to be here because coming to the Downtown Eastside changed my life and taught me some of the most profound lessons I've ever learned."

In his youth, Hari once attempted to revive a relative of his who had been using drugs, but the relative never woke up. That pain repeated itself when an adult Hari realized the depths of a partner's heroin and crack-cocaine use. He wanted to understand addiction, and this book was how he would do that.

Hari began writing when the 100-year anniversary of the first ban on drugs in 1914 was approaching: he was looking for answers to what he called, "really simple" questions including "Why did we go to war against people with addictions a hundred years ago? Why are we carrying on when it doesn't seem to work?" and, "What really causes addiction?"

The importance of connection

Here in Vancouver was where Hari first witnessed key breakthroughs in his understanding of addiction. The first provided the answer to what truly causes addiction.

The initial studies done on heroin, early in the 20th century, determined that the drug itself induced the compulsion. "You take a rat, you put it in a cage, and you give it two water bottles," Hari renders. "One is just water, and the other is [laced with] either heroin or cocaine. If you do that, the rat will almost always prefer the drugged water and almost always kill itself quite quickly," as a result, Hari said.

Vancouver's own Dr. Bruce Alexander, a retired professor of psychology at Simon Fraser University, told Hari that the more people he worked with on the Downtown Eastside, the more it occurred to him that there was something missing in these earlier studies.

"They're putting this rat alone in an empty cage, [with] none of the things that rats need to have a good life; they've got nothing to do except these drugs." Dr. Alexander replicated the experiment, but with a bigger cage, famously termed Rat Park, a 'heaven for rats', dubbs Hari. They're given others to socialize with, a partner to mate with, plenty cheese, and a couple balls to keep them active. "In Rat Park," notes Hari of the water bottle fortified with morphine, "none of them use it compulsively, and none of them ever overdose."

They went from almost 100 per cent compulsive use and overdose to none, says the UK journalist.

"The opposite of addiction is not sobriety, the opposite of addiction is connection." Hari is well known for penning. The core of addiction, he tells his Vancouver audience, is about life being too unbearable to be present in because it's too painful of a place to be.

Hari makes sure to note that we can't rule out the chemical aspect of addiction. Certain drugs, he says, hook onto brain receptors that exist for our natural neurochemicals, but this is only a tiny fraction of the picture, he asserts. When nicotine patches became commercially available in the early '90s, people were optimistic about a reduction in smoking. A nicotine patch, Hari says, delivers "all of the chemical equivalent" as smoking a cigarette does. Although some critics contest the experiment's results, the overall findings that addiction is rooted in more than just the chemical component of a drug resonated with a wide audience.

Punishment is ineffective

One of the core theories the War on Drugs is based on is that people with addiction need to be punished and made to suffer in order to give them the "incentive" to stop, Hari says. "But once you understand that pain is the cause of addiction, says Hari, you understand why inflicting *more* pain doesn't just, not work, it actually makes the problem worse."

Describing his visit to an Arizona prison, Hari says the inmates were "absolutely terrified of something called 'The Hole'. When shown this solitary confinement center by a prison guard, he saw a woman alone in a concrete cell with no windows and a single toilet. Trying to relay the magnitude of the horror he felt from this place, Hari describes the moment he realized this 'Hole' was, the closest thing [he'd] seen to a "literal, human reenactment of the cages that *guaranteed addiction* in rats," he says. "And this is what we're doing to these women thinking it will stop them from being addicted."

In person, the multiple award-winning journalist is surprisingly lighthearted and humorous for having covered such heavy subject matter for so many years. Hari details for the crowd a decades-old conversation between Portuguese Prime Minister and the leader of the opposition at the time. Realizing their country's crime surge couldn't go on, they "decided to do something super radical: something nobody had done in 70 years." Hari mimics them in a comical, air-headed tone: "Should we, like, ask some scientists and experts and stuff?", to which the audience erupted in laughter.

Telling this story of how Portugal significantly decreased what was once an unraveling problem in the year 2000, Hari continues in a more serious tone. By following the US model of increased arrest and imprisonment, they watched the problem get worse every year. So when those leaders hired experts whose panel made recommendations based on Dr. Bruce Alexander's Rat Park study, they decriminalized all drugs, "from cannabis to crack. The whole lot." Hari says.

The essential next step was to spend all their prosecution money on turning drug users lives around. Housing initiatives and microloan programs were created so people could start businesses from the things they cared about. "The goal was to say to everyone with addiction in Portugal," Hari says, "we value you; you've got as much right to a good life as anyone." When he arrived in Portugal 13 years later, drug injection had fallen by 50 per cent. Overdose deaths, HIV transmission, and street crime had all "massively" declined, he recalls.

Legalization can restore order: Hari

Hari describes how at the same time, a similar story was unfolding in Switzerland: crackdowns had resulted in increased problems. Oscillating between author and comedian, Hari emphasizes that the Swiss aren't particularly liberal, "[they're] obsessed with order," he teases.

Still yet, under the country's female president Ruth Dreifuss, Hari chronicles how the Swiss established therapy programs, job assistance, housing, and safe injection sites. "They give you the drug you're addicted to in the [purest] possible form", as well as a means to "figure out why you're in such pain, and to deal with the causes of pain." There was no pressure to cut back or stop the program, yet almost everyone does, Hari informs his listeners.

The results in Switzerland are very clear, the crowd hears. "More people have died in North America of opioid overdose since I started talking to you than have died in more than a decade in Switzerland."

124

"Legalization is the way to restore order to this chaos," Hari quotes of president Dreifuss upon stepping over the threshold at the beginning of the millennium.

Portugal, Switzerland (and even Sao Paulo, Brazil where Hari also visited) succeeded in reducing crime and addiction by dealing with the underlying causes of the pain, the reporter says. "And that's what we need to be thinking about".

Painkillers and emotional pain

The UK columnist details how a large proportion of Canadian women take drugs to treat depression. He notes that an extraordinary amount of people are "drugging themselves to get through the day." And the pain goes deep, he urges.

The well-researched journalist brings up Vancouver's renowned Dr. Gabor Maté, a physician who worked with The Portland Hotel Society. After listening to his patients (an anomaly in typical medical care), Maté described to Hari how he realized, "everyone at the PHS had been damaged horribly, long before they found their drug. The drug was an attempted solution to this very deep trauma."

Hari's talk includes a handful of personal stories as anecdotes to confirm Maté's theory. Recounting a woman in San Diego who had succeeded in a weight-loss program that cut back her overeating, Hari says she reached a healthy 150 pounds. But when she was hit by her partner, her binge eating returned. The doctors questioned when she first started to gain weight, and she replied: 12 years old, Hari recalls. When they pressed what else happened at that time, she answered, "Well, that was when my grandfather started to rape me."

In the 1990s, a woman named Liz Evans was working in a Downtown Eastside psychiatric unit. She realized that people were being thrown out of their housing for drug use. "Nobody's going to stop being addicted under a bridge - that's when [the addiction] is going to spiral," Hari recounts his meeting with Evans. She suggested unconditional housing, but authorities reacted badly.

One woman was given a room after being thrown out of housing for using drugs and selling sex, Hari recounts. "She would often come back beaten up, and she would tell Liz, 'I deserve this'." Her youth was spent cycling through foster care; one family starved her for a whole year and told her she was "diseased." Evans thought this woman had been punished enough, told her she didn't deserve to be beaten, and then just listened. "No one had ever said, 'tell me about your life, tell me about your pain'," Hari says.

The visiting correspondent proclaims that through the lens of the War on Drugs, "that story is a failure: [she] never stopped using drugs." The woman passed at 48. "But if you see it from a different perspective, it's a success. She didn't die on the streets ... She died in a room she was really proud of, reunited with her family on the Reservation where they took her [from]; she died surrounded by people who kept telling her they loved her. I don't think that's a failure, I think that's a success."

Addiction isn't a pathology, but more a grab at a solution, Hari maintains.

It's this insight that came from the Downtown Eastside and the work of those fighting for decency and human rights for people who have already been traumatized enough, that has resulted in such dramatic changes around the world Hari tells us. He reminds his Vancouver audience once again that we should be proud of our home. "The Downtown Eastside was a pioneer of Harm Reduction," Hari praises.

"I was told that, apparently in nature, the antidote is always found very close to a poison: they evolved together, they're twinned. Here in the Downtown Eastside, we see the wound most clearly," Hari says, "but we also see the beginnings of solutions, answers, and understanding; the way out of this."

"ADDICTION IS A MULTI-DIMENSIONAL PUBLIC HEALTH ISSUE"
--Khamdullahpur, McGill's Blogs, under "Drugs," 2-8-16

Stop telling me 'Everything you think you know about addiction is wrong'

You may have heard Johann Hari declare that 'everything we think we know about addiction is wrong' in his Ted talk of the same name (with nearly 4 million views), or his Huffington post article ambitiously titled "The Likely Cause of Addiction Has Been Discovered, and It Is Not What You Think". Hari emphasizes the need to move away from punishing individuals struggling with addiction and work on compassion and establishing meaningful human connections. Although this is a good message, the talk as a whole is deeply misguided, and filled with inaccurate, overly simplified and categorical information that is misleading. This is largely because Hari is a journalist by training and not a scientist or addiction specialist. Unfortunately he dismisses decades of important research into the neurobiological and genetic components of addiction (Goldman et al., 2005; Koob & Volkow, 2010).

He conjectures that environment and a lack of human connection are to blame for addiction, citing Bruce Alexander's Rat Park experiment and the return of veterans from the Vietnam War. Few who have experienced addiction or worked in the field would discount the significant role of environment, however it is reckless to discount decades of research in to its biological components. His primary evidence, the Rat Park experiment – which simply put, demonstrated that when morphine-addicted rats were placed in enriched environments they would not drink morphine-laced water – has never been replicated and does nothing to refute neuroimaging research showing that long lasting impairments in decision-making are still present long after abstinence has been achieved (Goldstein & Volkow, 2011). Hari also implies Vietnam veterans came home and easily ceased using heroin, failing to mention that all returning soldiers had to complete urine screens and, if necessary, detoxification before returning to the United States. In addition, he fails to acknowledge that potential soldiers with mental illness were not drafted (Robins et al., 2010). This is extremely important given that concurrent psychiatric illness is very prevalent among heroin users, and is often a key predictor of failure to improve from treatment (Coupland et al., 2014).

The most surprising moment of Hari's talk, however, is when he argues that if addiction was strongly rooted in biology, people who are given painkillers post-surgery or after an injury would become addicted; "you will have noticed if your grandmother had a hip replacement, she didn't come out as a junkie". You can only conclude that Johann Hari is clearly unfamiliar with the ongoing prescription opioid epidemic which in 2014 claimed the lives of nearly 20,000 people in the United States alone (NIH, 2015). This does not reflect well on Hari's evaluation of the scientific literature, or his three and a half year, 30,000-mile journey to better understand addiction.

Johan Hari's work on addiction is a good example of the dangers of a little bit of knowledge. He makes unsubstantiated, sweeping statements without any critical appraisal of his own conclusions. It is dangerous to preach such a restrictive ideology about what is likely one of the world's most multi-dimensional public health issues. Ignoring the biological aspect of addiction will only serve to limit the insight and understanding of those struggling with drug and alcohol abuse. What do you think?

CONCLUSION

ADOPTEES, in particular, have been telling us how and why they became drug addicted to self-medicate their pain from feelings of rejection, grief from loss, fear of secondary abandonment, distrust, and adversarial biological-adoptive parent relationships imposed by state law in sealed adoption. But have we been listening? Is it so difficult to understand that the hardest part of the "multi-dimensional issue" of addiction for *any* addict is confronting such feelings without support? Although faith-based rehabilitation and recovery programs may "be there" to support an substance abuser wishing to quit alcohol or drugs, the program reinforces the idea that they are still and always will be an alcoholic or addict who happens to be abstaining. Other programs believe that addiction results from one of four causes (or some combination thereof):

1. Chemical imbalance;

2. Unresolved events from the past;

3. Beliefs people hold that are inconsistent with what is true; and

4. The inability to cope with current conditions.

So treatment entails medical, psychological, and emotional support (connecting).

RESOURCES DIRECTORY

ADOPTION DISCLOSURE LAWS
The Ultimate Search Book
LoriCarangelo.com/UltimateSearch

ADOPTION LAWS BY STATE
bastards.org/activism/access.htm

ADOPTIVE PARENTS FOR OPEN RECORDS
and AGAINST ADOPTION
Facebook.com/Anti-AdoptionAdopters

ALANON / ALATEEN
Al-Anon-Alateen.org
wso@al-anon.org

AMERICAN ADOPTION CONGRESS
1-202-483-3399
-see website for local contact
http://americanadoptioncongress.org

AMERICAN BAR ASSOCIATION
740 -15th St, NW Washington, DC 20005-1019
1-202-662-1000
http://aba.net

AMERICAN CIVIL LIBERTIES UNION (ACLU)
125 Broad Street, 18th Floor
New York, NY 10004
(212) 549-2500
http://aclu.org

AMERICA'S PROMISE Mentors
900 Washington St., Ste 400
Alexandria, VA 22314
america'spromise.org
local@america'spromise.org
1-888-559-6884

BARBARA SINATRA
CHILDREN'S CENTER
39000 Bob Hope Drive
Rancho Mirage, CA 92270
1-760-340-2336
BarbaraSinatraChildrensCenter.org

BASTARD NATION
PO Box 1469
Edmond, OK 73083-1469
http://bastards.org

BIG BROTHERS/BIG SISTERS
230 North 13th Street
Philadelphia, PA 19107
1-215-567-7000
http://bbbs.org

CARLIS, Tracy I., PhD
Adoption/Death Penalty expert
Carlis Psychological Services Inc.
16430 Ventura Blvd Suite 203
Encino, Calif. 91436
www.drtracylcarlis.com
drcarlis@drtracylcarlis.com
(818)713-0508

CHILD WELFARE INFORMATION GATEWAY
(Federal government website)
childwelfare.gov

CHILDHELP USA (National HQ)
for child abuse prevention,
residential treatment villages, foster care
15757 North 78th Street, Ste. B Scottsdale, AZ 85260
1-800-4-A-CHILD - 24 hr. Hotline
1-480-922-8212
http://childhelp.org

CHILDREN OF THE NIGHT
1450 Sylvan Street
Van Nuys, CA 91411
1-800-551-1300 - Hotline
1-818-908-4474 –Main
llee@childrenofthenight.org

CONCERNED UNITED BIRTHPARENTS (CUB, Inc)
PO Box 341442
Los Angeles, CA 90034-9442
1-800-822-2777
info@CUBirthparents.org

CPS WATCH INC.
PO Box 974
Branson, MO 65615-0974
1-888-CPS-WATCH
http://cpswatch.com

CAL FARLEY'S BOYS RANCH
and GIRLS TOWN USA PO Box 1890
Amarillo, TX 79174-0001
1-800-687-3722
http://calfarley.org ; info@calfarley.org

DAVID KIRSCHNER, PhD,
Clinical Psychology (Expert Witness)
44 Juneau Blvd., Woodbury, NY 11797
1-516-692-6060 DK21544808@aol.com

DATE OF BIRTH SEARCH
DOBSearch.com

DELANCEY STREET FOUNDATION
(Model substance abuse/ex-con prog)
600 Embarcadero
San Francisco, CA 94017
http://DelanceySreetFoundation.org

DNA TESTING and MATCHING-
23&Me.com

FAMILIES AGAINST MANDATORY MINIMUMS
1612 "K" Street, NW, Ste. #700
Washington, DC 20006
1-202-822-6700
http://famm.org

FATHER FLANAGAN'S BOYS TOWN
13603 Flanagan Blvd. Boys Town, NE 68010
National Hotline: 1-800-448-3000
http://boystown.org
hotline@boystown.org

GENESIS HOUSE
621 - 34th Avenue / PO Box 22910
Seattle, WA 98122
1-206-328-0881
http://genesishouse.com
info@genesishouse.com

HOMEBUILDERS PROGRAM INSTITUTE
34004 - 16th Ave South, Ste# 200
Federal Way, WA 98003-8903–HQ
1-253-874-3630-Seattle; 1-253-927-1550-Tacoma
http://strengtheningfamilies.org

HOMELESS SHELTERS DIRECTORY-U.S.
http://homelessshelterdirectory.org

HOMES NOT JAILS (meeting room)
1-877-50-SQUAT (773828)
c/o Housing Rights Committee San Francisco
417 South Van Ness Ave (at 15th St)
San Francisco, CA 94103
1-415-713-8634 (HRC)
http://homesnotjails.org
contact@homesnotjails.org

HOUSE OF RUTH
2201 Argonne Drive
Baltimore, MD 21218
1-410-889-0840-admin office
1-410-889-RUTH (7884)-24-HR Hotline
http://hruth.org
info@hruth.org

IDENTIGENE
DNA-Paternity, Relationship Testing
1-800-404-GENE-toll free;
http://dnatesting.com

INNOCENCE PROJECT
Benjamin N.Cardozo School of Law
55 – 5th Ave, 11th Floor
New York City, New York 10003
innocenceproject.org
info@innocenceproject.org

INTERNATIONAL SOUNDEX REUNION REGISTRY (ISRR)
PO Box 2312
Carson City, NV 89701
http://isrr.net

NATIONAL ADOPTION INFORMATION
CLEARINGHOUSE (NAIC)
1250 Maryland Ave, SW, 8th Fl
Washington, DC 20024
1-800-394-3366-toll free;
http://childwelfare.gov/

NATIONAL ASSOC. OF WORKFORCE BOARDS (NAWB)
& PRIVATE INDUSTRY COUNCILS (NAPIC)
1133 - 19th Street, NW, 2nd Floor
Washington, DC 20005
1-202-289-2950
http://nawb.org

NATIONAL CENTER FOR MISSING AND
EXPLOITED CHILDREN (NCMEC)
Charles B. Wang International Bldg.
699 Prince Street
Alexandria, VA 22314-3175
1-800-THE-LOST (1-800-843-5678)
1-703-224-2150-phone;
1-703-224-2122-FAX
http://missingkids.com/

NATIONAL CRIMINAL JUSTICE
REFERENCE SERVICE (NCJRS)
(A-Z Topics Links)
http://ncjrs.gov/viewall.html

PASSAGES MALIBU
(Non-12-step Substance Abuse
Treatment, in Malibu & Ventura, CA)
1-866-560-3530
http://passagesmalibu.com

PRISONER LOCATOR (Free)
http://ancestorhunt.com/prison_search.htm

PRISONER LOCATOR - CALIFORNIA (Free)
http://inmatelocator.cdcr.ca.gov

PRISONER SUPPORT DIRECTORY (Free)
PO Box 339
Berkeley, CA 94701 (510)893-4648
http://prisonactivist.com

SALVATION ARMY HQ
615 Slaters Lane
PO Box 269
Alexandria, VA 22313;
http://salvationarmyusa.org

SOS CHILDREN'S VILLAGES Pompano Beach, FL 33060 http://sos.bc.or
(Worldwide link) http://sosflorida.com (FL project)

STANFORD UNIV MILLS CRIMINAL DEFENSE CLINIC (for CA "Three
Strikes"/ Life cases)
559 Nathan Abbott Way
Stanford, CA 94305

SOUTHERN POVERTY LAW CTR
400 Washington Avenue
Montgomery, AL 36104
1-334-956-8200
http://splcenter.org

ULTIMATE SEARCH BOOK, THE
U.S and Worldwide Editions
https://www.amazon.com/dp/0942605691/

UNITED NATIONS CONVENTION ON RIGHTS OF THE CHILD
Najat Maalla M'jid, Spec Rapporteur
UN Centre, Palais des Nations
CH-1211 Geneva 10, Switzerland
http://unicef.org

WOMEN'S ALTERNATIVE CENTER PROGRAM
225 S Chester Rd, #6
Swathmore, Pennsylvania 19081
womensassoc.org
(610) 543-5022

BIBLIOGRAPHY

Akafat, Roman, *"International Adoption Corruption" What You Must Know Before You Adopt a Child or Children,"* Amazon, 2015

Austin, Linda Tollet, *"Babies For Sale: The Tennessee Children's Home,"* Greenwood Press, 1993.

Benet, Mary K., *"The Politics of Adoption,"* The Free Press, 1976

Bloom, Dr. Lee, *"Growing Up Behind Locked Doors,"* Rolling Stone Magazine, 1986.

Bowlby, John., *"Illegitimacy and Deprivation,"* World Health Organization, Maternal Care and Mental Health Monograph Series 4, 2nd ed., 115,149,152; and *"Child Mourning and It's Implications for Psychiatry,"* American Journal of Psychiatry, The Alfred Mayer Lecture, p.481-498, 1961.

Cadoret, Remi, *"Biologic Perspectives of Adoptee Adjustment,"* (Brodzinsky), Oxford Press University , 1990.

Carp, E. Wayne, *"Jean Paton and the Struggle to Reform American Adoption,"* University of Michigan Press, 2014.

Chesler, Phyillis, *"Sacred Bond,"* and *"Mothers On Trial,"* 1986

CNN News, *"More Than 2000 Wrongfully Convicted People Exonerated in 23 Years, Researchers Say,"* 5-31-12.

Coles, Gary, *"The Invisible Men of Adoption,"* BookPOD, 2011.

Colevecchio-Van Sickler, *"Man Shoots Girlfriend, Rapes Girl, Then Kills Self,"* St. Petersburg Times, 8-18-04

D'Arcy, Claudia Corrigan, *"National Council For Adoption: Mothers, Money Marketing and Madness,"* Musings of the Lame, 2017.

Diver, Alice, *"A Law of Blood Ties: The Right to Access Genetic Ancestry,"* Springer Verlag, 2013"

Domingues, Joel Lee, interview and correspondence with Lori Carangelo, 2005 through 2007

Donalds, Elizabeth S., *"Voices of Adoptees: Stories and Experiences Within the Schools,"* Dissertation, Antioch University-New England, 2012.

Fariris, Theresa Rodrigues, *"When Adoption Fails,"* Housekeeper Publishing, 2008.

Fessler, Ann, *"The Girls Who Went Away,"* Penguin Books, 2007; and *"A Girl Like Her,"* (motion picture), LEF Foundation, Moving Image Fund, 2012.

FindLaw, *"Domingues v. State,"* Georgia Supreme Court No. S03A1458, 12-17-03

Fisher, Nancy L, MD, MPH, "*Cultural and Ethnic Diversity: A Guide for Genetics Professionals,*" John Hopkins University Press, 1966.

Fletcher, Sybil Lash, "*Supreme Deception,*" Sentinel Productions. 2002 Death Data, and Dekalb County Vital Records

Goldstein, L.A. and Carol R., "*Beyond the Best Interests of the Child,*" Free Press, 1972

Goodman, Peter S., "*Stealing Babies for Adoption,*" Washington Post Foreign Service, 3-12-06.

Griffith, Keith, "*The Right to Know Who You Are,*" Katherine Kimball Publishing, 1992.

Hallowell, Billy, "*Meet Mary Doe...*" The Blaze, http://theblaze.com, 1-25-13

Hari, Johann, "*Chasing the Scream: The First and Last Days of the War on Drugs*" ["*The Opposite of Addiction is Connection*"], Bloomberg USA, 2015

Hayes, John, "*Theft By Adoption,*" Amazon Books, 7-14-08.

Hood, G., "*Adoption or Abduction?*" Dan Rather Reports, AXS TV, 2012

Inglis, K., "*Living Mistakes: Mothers Who Consented to Adoption,*" G.Allen & Unwin, 1984

Innocence Project, "*Facts and Figures,*" FalseConfessions.org

Jalsevac, John, '*Two Women Are Behind Legal Abortion in America; Now Both of Them Want It Reversed,*" Lifestyle News, 1-17-13

Joyce, Kathryn, "*The Child Catcher: Rescue, Trafficking and the New Gospel of Adoption,*" Public Affairs, 2013

Kirk, H. David, "*Shared Fate: The Theory of Adoption and Mental Health,*" The Free Press of Glencoe, 1994.

Kirschner, David, Phd, "*Adoption Forensics: The Connection Between Adoption and Murder,*" Crime Magazine, 2007; and "*The Adopted Child Syndrome: Considerations for Psychotherapy,*" Adelphi Society, 1978,

Lahl, Jennifer, "*Baby Market As Financial Market,*" Center for Bioethics and Culture, 2016.

National Council For Adoption (NCFA), reference to "*culture of adoption,*" NCFA website

Reagan, Michael, "*On the Outside Looking In,*" Zebra, 1988.

Riben, Marsha, "*Shedding Light on the Dark Side of Adoption,*" Harlo Press, 1988

Samuels, Elizabeth, "*How Adoption in America Grew Secret,*" Washington Post, 2001.

Sawyer, Josh, "*Death By Adoption*," Cicada Press, 2014.

Solinger, Rickie, "*Pregnancy and Power: A History of Reproductive Politics in America*"

Verrier, Nancy Newton, "*Primal Wound: Understanding the Adopted Child*," Gateway Press, 2003.

Walker, Leslie: "*A Sudden Fury: A True Story of Adoption and Murder*," St. Martin's Press, 1989

Walsh, Lauren, "*Exclusive: Prison Guard Caught at Work with Drugs, Charged with Intent to Distribute*," NBC-26 TV News 7-13-12; also Augusta Chronicle, and WAG-TV News-Atlanta, 7-13-12

Weigel, Margaret and John Whitby, "*False Confessions, New Data and Law Enforcement Interrogations: Research Findings*," JournalistsResource.org, 1-15-15

Wellisch, E., "*Children Without Genealogy – A Problem of Adoption*," Mental Health 13, 1952.

Wilson-Buterbaugh, Karen, "*The Baby Scoop Era: Unwed Mothers, Infant Adoption and Forced Surrender*," Amazon Books, 2017.

INDEX

ABOUT THE AUTHOR

Lori Carangelo is retired from 25 years of administrative positions in Santa Barbara and Palm Desert, California, where she authored over 600 published articles and 22 unique non-fiction, adoption-themed and true crime books available on Amazon.

Her adoption-themed books result from her adoption reform activism and the thousands of adoptee-birth family reunions that she and her national volunteer network, Americans For Open Records (AmFOR), facilitated without charge. Using the data gleaned from those reunions and additional research, she served a Data Source to the United Nations Rights of the Child Project and its "Sale of Children" Report.

Her "true crime" books endeavor to explain WHY they did it.

Also by Lori Carangelo

SCHOOL SHOOTERS
How and Why They Did It
And America's War on Guns

CHOSEN CHILDREN
People, Politics and America's Failed
Foster Care and Adoption Industries

ADOPTION UNCENSORED
4 Decades of Politics, People and Commentary

THE ULTIMATE SEARCH BOOK
U.S. and Worldwide Editions

THE ADOPTION AND DONOR CONCEPTION FACTBOOK
The Only Comprehensive Source of U.S. & Global Data
on the Hidden Families of Foster Care, Adoption and Donor Conception

SERIAL KILLERS ON THE INTERSTATE -
200 Highway Killers by State

ADOPTED KILLERS
430 Adoptees Who Killed – How and Why They Did It

KONDRO
The "Uncle Joe" Killer

JAMES MUNRO –
And the Freeway Killers

EYEWITNESS!
The Carefully Crafted Central Coast Rapist

RAGE!
How An Adoption Ignited A Fire

ESPOSITO
The First Mafioso

Made in the USA
Middletown, DE
08 July 2023